Naturally, DELICIOUS

DESSERTS

Naturally, DELICIOUS

DESSERTS

100 SWEET BUT NOT SINFUL TREATS

Danny Seo

From the kitchens of *Naturally, Danny Seo*

GIBBS SMITH
TO ENRICH AND INSPIRE HUMANKIND

To Kerry.
You're the sweetest thing.

First Edition
24 23 22 21 20   5 4 3 2 1

Text © 2020 Danny Seo
Photographs by Alexandra Grablewski: pages 21, 23, 58, 63, 64, 67, 83, 84, 87, 88, 91, 92, 95, 100, 113, 115, 117, 118, 138, 152, 155, 156, 159, 160, 162, 170, 173, 177, 178, 181, 182, 185, 186, 192, 194, 197, 202, 205, 206, 209, 210
Photographs by Armando Rafael: pages 13, 99, 103, 108, 130, 133, 134, 141, 142, 165, 166
Photographs by David Engelhardt: pages 14, 17, 18, 96, 164, 174, 191, 213
Photographs by Rikki Snyder: pages 8, 10, 24, 27, 28, 31, 32, 35, 36, 39, 41, 42, 45, 47, 51, 53, 54, 57, 60, 68, 71, 72, 75, 76, 79, 80, 105, 107, 111, 121, 123, 125, 126, 129, 145, 146, 149, 151, 188, 198, 201, 214, 217, 218, and front cover
Photographs by Shelly Strazis: page 137
Photograph by Victoria Pearson: page 7

Published by
Gibbs Smith
P.O. Box 667
Layton, Utah 84041

1.800.835.4993 orders
www.gibbs-smith.com

Designed by Made Visible Studio
Printed and bound in China
Gibbs Smith books are printed on either recycled, 100% post-consumer waste, FSC-certified papers or on paper produced from sustainable PEFC-certified forest/controlled wood source. Learn more at www.pefc.org.

Library of Congress Control Number: 2020933150
ISBN: 978–1–4236–5537–4

CONTENTS

ACKNOWLEDGMENTS

It sure takes a village to make a book and this is no exception.

Of course, a big dose of gratitude goes to Gibbs Smith and my editor Michelle Branson who had the brilliant idea to turn my love of desserts with a healthy twist into a book.

My agent I've worked with for as long as I can remember—Joy Tutela—who has been a guide, a friend and—like the Golden Girls jingle says—a confidant.

The hardworking photographers who contributed to this book: Alexandra Grablewski, Rikki Snyder, David Engelhardt, Armando Rafael, and Shelly Strazis.

In my earlier life, I was a prop stylist, so I can appreciate what it takes to turn a simple recipe into a work-of-art in photos. Here's a big cheer to the stylists who worked on these images: Maeve Sheridan, Kristine Trevino, Nidia Cuevo, Corey Belle, Eugene Jho, and Leslie Orlandi.

Plus everyone at the magazine who help churn out one issue after another (and each time better!): Sandy Soria, Alexis Cook, Mike Wilson, and all the contributing writers and everyone at RFP Corp who help behind the scenes. And to all the brand partners who have supported us from the start and continue to do so today, thank you soooo much.

And finally, a big thank you to all the viewers and readers. It's one thing to create a beautiful product, but it's only worth it when it inspires and excites people like you. I do this for you. Cheers!

INTRODUCTION

The funny thing is, I have never really been a person with a "sweet tooth." In fact, I am more likely to decline dessert and opt for an extra serving of something salty, crispy, and savory over something sugary, creamy, and rich.

So you might be reading this and wondering: Why on earth did you write a book on desserts then? Because, when I do have a rare hankering for something sweet, I basically live by this motto: *just go for it.*

But it's not an all-you-can-eat binge fest on sugar and fat. Instead, they're actual desserts that still have the *Naturally* ethos of adding in nutrition (like veggies and high fiber grains), using real, wholesome ingredients, and steering clear of artificial flavors and colors in the recipes. They're worth the calories and lightened up just enough to lessen the guilt.

And these desserts have to be worth the time to make, too. In an increasingly busy world, I wanted all of the recipes to be simple, but not dumbed down. Just that right balance of being able to look at all the steps and ingredients and come to a conclusion that you could make it and you could make it right. No hard-to-find ingredients and no special tools only a James Beard-worthy pastry chef would have in their arsenal.

What is in *Naturally, Delicious Desserts* is a compendium of my top 100 sweet treats we've published in the pages of the magazine. I've also baked many of these on the set of my TV show, so if you've watched and didn't have a pen and paper handy, now you've got one place to find all of those recipes. There's also enough variety and ideas here for you to find a treasure trove of new favorites and to be inspired to lighten some old-fashioned recipes you might have that are passed down from generation to generation. I mean, who knew you could make your own Twix bars that taste better than the store-bought version? Or slip eggplant into brownies because it makes it fudgier and just better? And who wouldn't love giant blue marshmallows to garnish a piping hot cup of coffee or toasted and melted in between graham crackers and chocolate? Oh, yeah . . . you can make your own marshmallows, and it's easy, too!

I'm definitely a friend of desserts, not a fiend. And when you try something from this book, I hope you'll find they are friendly for your health, friendly for the planet and—yes—will make friends to satisfy your sweet tooth, too.

Let's celebrate something sweet together.

-DANNY SEO

JUST COOKIES

Who am I talking about here? He says, "me want cookie!" or "me eat cookie!" or how about just "Om nom nom nom!" Yes, of course I'm talking about the Cookie Monster.

And it's easy to understanding why. Cookies are delicious! They are easy to make and you can make big batches of them to eat warm out of the oven and save the rest to eat in the future. I LOVE cookies. And I'll guess you're with me if the following words mean something to you: Thin Mints, Tagalongs, and Do-Si-Dos. Folks, *Troop Beverly Hills* wasn't my favorite childhood movie for the cinematography—it was for the fact those boxes of cookies were the STAR of that film.

But let's face it, man cannot live on cookies alone because it's not part of a well-balanced meal. *We all know that.* And for those fake "healthy" cookies that are high in protein, low in carbs, and have zero sugar, you, sir, are no cookie. You may be shaped like one, but you are what's considered a round disc that's a distant cousin of corrugated cardboard.

So this chapter is what our crazy culinary team at *Naturally* came up with to satisfy my sweet tooth and make me feel a little less guilty in my indulgence. There are no diet fake-outs here. You see, these cookie recipes use real ingredients to make really good treats. But we've also swapped in clever things like vegetables (seriously, you'd never know) and all-natural sweeteners to replace processed sugar. And because we all have busy lives, they're fast and easy to make. No piping bags. No French molds. No special trip to Williams Sonoma to get anything you don't already have. Crunchy, crispy, and chewy . . . it's all here.

The Famous Friday Chocolate Chip Cookies

MAKES 48 COOKIES

Every year, I go to this wellness spa in Mexico called Rancho La Puerta and do plenty of rigorous workouts, drink tons of water, and lay off the booze. The food there is also very healthy. But on Fridays there's a treat, and it's these insanely chewy chocolate chip cookies. After many years of asking for the recipe, I was able to get my hands on it and share it with you!

GATHER

1 cup unsalted butter, softened

½ cup firmly packed brown sugar

2 eggs

1 cup milk

2 cups rolled oats

1 cup wheat germ

1 cup wheat flake cereal

1 cup white whole-wheat flour or whole-wheat pastry flour

1 cup sliced almonds

1 teaspoon cinnamon

1 teaspoon baking powder

½ teaspoon baking soda

1 cup semisweet chocolate chips

½ cup dried cranberries, chopped

48 chocolate kisses, unwrapped

MAKE IT

1. Preheat the oven to 350°F.

2. In a stand mixer fitted with the paddle attachment, cream the butter and brown sugar. Add the eggs, 1 at a time, then the milk, beating until combined. (The milk will not quite combine with the butter well and the mixture will look a little separated, but this is fine.)

3. In a separate bowl, combine the oats, wheat germ, cereal, flour, almonds, cinnamon, baking powder, and baking soda. Add the chocolate chips and cranberries.

4. Add oat mixture to the milk mixture, and mix on the lowest speed until thoroughly combined.

5. Use a tablespoon measure or small ice cream scoop to scoop the dough onto lightly oiled baking sheets, leaving 2 inches between each scoop.

6. Press a chocolate kiss into the center of each cookie.

7. Bake for 14 minutes, or until lightly browned.

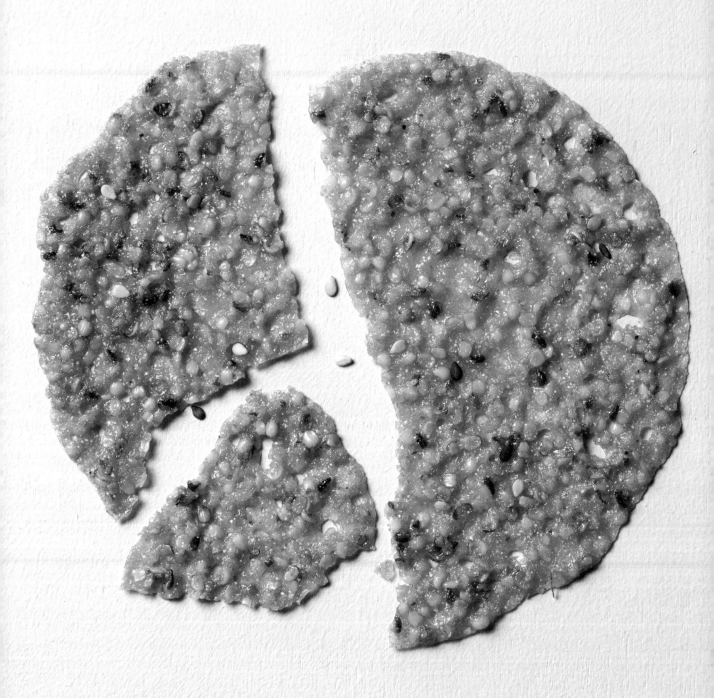

Lemon-Scented Hemp Seed Lace Cookies

MAKES 12 COOKIES

These delicate, crispy, and caramelized cookies are always a hit. They are also fantastic crumbled up on vanilla ice cream. By the way, if you don't have a Silpat sheet, you can also use unbleached parchment paper. Don't go without using; you won't be able to gently pry them off an unlined cookie sheet.

GATHER

¼ cup hemp seeds

2½ tablespoons whole-wheat pastry flour

1 tablespoon arrowroot powder

1 tablespoon melted coconut oil

2 tablespoons brown rice syrup

2½ tablespoons maple syrup

½ teaspoon lemon extract

Pinch of sea salt

MAKE IT

1. Preheat oven to 350°F. Line baking sheets with Silpat. Add hemp seeds, flour, and arrowroot to a medium bowl. Whisk to combine.

2. In separate bowl, whisk oil, rice syrup, maple syrup, lemon extract, and salt until thoroughly combined. Add to hemp mixture, mixing just until moistened. Let batter rest for 15 minutes.

3. Use a teaspoon to drop batter onto baking sheets, leaving space between cookies to allow spreading. Bake for 10 minutes until cookies are bubbly. Let cookies cool for approximately 30 seconds before removing onto wire rack.

Black and White Sesame Cookies

MAKES APPROXIMATELY 20 COOKIES

Sesame seeds are one of the original "superfoods." They have two unique ingredients called sesamin and seamol, which have been shown to induce cholesterol reduction in a number of studies. It also has a strong nutty flavor that lends well in this sweet treat.

GATHER

- 1½ cups whole-wheat pastry flour (I like Bob's Red Mill)
- 1½ teaspoons baking powder
- ¼ teaspoon sea salt
- ¾ cup well-emulsified tahini
- ⅓ cup coconut oil, melted
- ½ cup maple syrup
- ½ teaspoon vanilla extract
- ¼ cup black and white sesame seeds

MAKE IT

1. Preheat oven to 350°F. Line 2 baking sheets with parchment paper.

2. In medium bowl, sift flour, baking powder, and salt together. In stand mixer, blend tahini, oil, maple syrup, and vanilla extract. Add flour mixture to tahini mixture in stand mixer and combine.

3. Using a 1-ounce scoop, form cookies onto baking sheets, sprinkle with sesame seeds, and press cookies down with back of fork.

4. Bake 10–15 minutes or until bottoms are golden brown. Remove cookies from pans to wire racks to cool.

Dark Chocolate–Ginger Macaroons

MAKES 14 TO 16 COOKIES

Yes, dark chocolate can be good for you. It's loaded with iron, magnesium, copper, zinc, and potassium. But as with most foods, these power-packed chewy, gooey, chocolate-y cookies should be eaten in moderation.

GATHER

½ cup semisweet dark chocolate pieces

Pinch of sea salt

2 large egg whites

½ cup plus 2 tablespoons maple crystals, ground

½ teaspoon vanilla extract

1 tablespoon ginger powder

1 cup unsweetened shredded coconut

3 tablespoons cocoa powder, sifted

MAKE IT

1. Preheat oven to 350°F. Line a baking sheet with parchment paper.

2. Using a double boiler, melt chocolate and set aside to cool.

3. In a medium bowl, add salt to egg whites and beat with electric mixer. Slowly add maple crystals to form soft peaks.

4. Using a spatula, fold in vanilla extract, ginger powder, and coconut. Add cocoa powder and cooled melted chocolate. Gently stir to incorporate all ingredients.

5. Using a 1-ounce scoop, scoop out cookies onto baking sheet leaving room for slight spread. Bake 15–20 minutes. Cool on wire racks.

Miniature Pink Raspberry Meringues

MAKES 12 TO 16 MERINGUES

Traditional meringues take hours in the oven, but can end with uneven results. Using a dehydrator works two ways to guarantee success: it delivers low and consistent heat and also blows out moisture. It's a winning way to make perfect meringues every time. If you don't have a dehydrator, it's a good time to turn to your social network and ask: it's worth the effort to borrow and give dehydrating a try.

GATHER

4   egg whites

½   teaspoon cream of tartar

2   cups organic evaporated cane juice

1   cup freeze-dried raspberries

MAKE IT

1. Add egg whites and cream of tartar to a large bowl.

2. Beat until soft peaks form then add sweetener, 1 tablespoon at a time, until meringue is stiff.

3. Crush the raspberries into a fine powder and gently fold into mixture. Transfer into a lined pastry bag fitted with a star tip and pipe mixture onto a teflex or silicone-lined dehydrator tray.

4. Dehydrate at 140°F for 4 hours, or until crisp.

Red, White, And Blue Coconut Macaroons

MAKES 12 MACAROONS

Coconut meat is loaded in folates, riboflavin, niacin, and thiamin.
Using a dehydrator helps preserve those vitamins,
so these sweet treats are actually good for you.

Strawberry Macaroons

GATHER

- 1 cup unsweetened, finely shredded coconut
- ½ cup coconut flour
- 2 tablespoons virgin coconut oil
- ¼ cup coconut nectar
- Pinch of sea salt
- ½ teaspoon strawberry extract
- ½ cup freeze-dried strawberries

MAKE IT

1. Mix the coconut flakes, coconut flour, coconut oil, coconut nectar, salt, and strawberry extract in a medium bowl.

2. Crush freeze-dried berries by passing through a strainer, and fold into mixture. Using an ice cream scoop or tablespoon measure, scoop mixture onto teflex or silicone-lined dehydrator tray.

3. Dehydrate for 4 hours at 115°F, or until the outside of the macaroon is slightly firm, but the inside is still soft.

Simply Coconut Macaroons

GATHER

- 1 cup unsweetened, finely shredded coconut
- ½ cup coconut flour
- 2 tablespoons virgin coconut oil
- ¼ cup coconut nectar
- Pinch of sea salt
- 1 teaspoon coconut extract

MAKE IT

1. Mix the coconut flakes, coconut flour, coconut oil, coconut nectar, salt, and coconut extract in a medium bowl.

2. Using an ice cream scoop or tablespoon measure, scoop mixture onto teflex or silicone-lined dehydrator tray.

3. Dehydrate for 4 hours at 115°F, or until the outside of the macaroon is slightly firm, but the inside is still soft.

Blueberry Macaroons

GATHER

1 cup unsweetened, finely shredded coconut

½ cup coconut flour

2 tablespoons virgin coconut oil

¼ cup coconut nectar

Pinch of sea salt

½ teaspoon almond extract

½ cup freeze-dried blueberries

MAKE IT

1. Mix the coconut flakes, coconut flour, coconut oil, coconut nectar, salt, and almond extract in a medium bowl.

2. Crush freeze-dried berries by passing through a strainer, and fold into mixture. Using an ice cream scoop or tablespoon measure, scoop mixture onto teflex or silicone-lined dehydrator tray.

3. Dehydrate for 4 hours at 115°F, or until the outside of the macaroon is slightly firm, but the inside is still soft.

Parsnip Oatmeal Raisin Cookies

MAKES 24 COOKIES

There's no need to overload desserts with added sugars when you use whole food sources like parsnips and raisins. Naturally sweet, parsnips are an instant match for these oatmeal raisin cookies. It doesn't hurt that they are also high in fiber, vitamin C, antioxidants, folic acid, and minerals including calcium and iron.

GATHER

WET INGREDIENTS

¾ cup organic unsalted butter, softened to room temperature

1 cup organic brown sugar

2 organic eggs

2 teaspoons vanilla extract

DRY INGREDIENTS

1½ cups whole-wheat flour

2 teaspoons ground cinnamon

1 tablespoon baking powder

½ teaspoon sea salt

2 cups rolled oats

ADD-INS

2 medium parsnips, peeled and core removed

¾ cup raisins

3 cups boiling water

MAKE IT

1. Add the butter and sugar to a large bowl. Use an electric mixer to beat the mixture for approximately 2 minutes or until fluffy.

2. Add in the eggs, 1 at a time, followed by the vanilla extract, and mix for additional minute.

3. In a separate bowl, sift in the flour, cinnamon, baking powder, and sea salt. Add in the oats, and stir to combine.

4. Using a food processor, pulse the parsnips until they form small, finely shredded pieces. Add to raisins, and cover mixture with boiling water. Allow to rest for 10 minutes. Drain thoroughly.

5. Slowly incorporate the dry ingredients into the wet ingredients, stirring with a rubber spatula until well combined. Fold the softened parsnips and raisins into the batter.

6. Chill cookie dough for 30 minutes in refrigerator.

7. In the meantime, preheat oven to 350°F and line baking sheets with parchment paper.

8. Scoop a heaping tablespoon of dough onto the baking sheet, flattening slightly and leaving 2 inches between each piece.

9. Bake for 12 minutes. Place on wire rack to set and cool.

Ready-To-Eat Maple Chocolate Chip Cookie Dough

MAKES 1 NICE SHAREABLE BOWL

We've been told as children to **never, ever** eat raw cookie dough
because it's not safe to eat due to raw eggs being in the mixture.
Well, we're not kids anymore, and this is a fully plant-based recipe that's delicious
all on its own. Stir into vanilla ice cream for the ultimate dessert.

GATHER

2   cups almond flour

1   cup oat flour

1/4   teaspoon sea salt

1/2   cup maple syrup

2   teaspoons vanilla extract

1/4   cup almond butter

1   cup miniature dark chocolate chips

MAKE IT

1. Sift the almond flour, oat flour, and salt in a medium bowl, and set aside.

2. In a separate bowl, whisk together the maple syrup, vanilla extract, and almond butter.

3. Add the maple mixture into the flour mixture, stirring until evenly combined.

4. Fold in chocolate chips. Refrigerate dough for 10–20 minutes, for a firmer texture.

Almond Butter Gingersnap Cookies

MAKES 12 COOKIES

This is a classic cookie with a modern makeover,
and it's the perfect one to whip up during the holiday season.
And guess what? This only takes 15 minutes to bake to perfection.

GATHER

1   cup creamy almond butter

1   cup coconut sugar

1   teaspoon baking powder

2   teaspoons ground ginger

1   teaspoon ground cinnamon

½   teaspoon ground cloves

    Pinch of sea salt

MAKE IT

1. Preheat oven to 350°F. Line a baking sheet with parchment paper.

2. In a medium bowl, add the almond butter and coconut sugar. Stir with a spoon or with hands until dough forms. Allow mixture to rest for 5 minutes.

3. Add the baking powder, ginger, cinnamon, cloves, and salt to the dough, using hands to evenly work in ingredients.

4. Scoop 2 tablespoons of cookie batter and press between palms of hands to form a circular disc, approximately $1/4$-inch thick.

5. Place formed cookie on baking sheet, and repeat with remaining batter, leaving space between each cookie.

6. Bake for 12 minutes then cool for a few minutes on the baking sheet before removing cookies and placing on a wire rack.

Holiday Paleo Thin Mints

MAKES 12 COOKIES

What's not to love? It tastes like a beloved Girl Scout cookie.
It's Paleo-friendly. And it has **chocolate**.

GATHER

1 cup almond flour

2 tablespoons cocoa powder

Pinch of sea salt

2 tablespoons coconut oil, melted

¼ cup maple syrup

1 teaspoon peppermint extract, or more to taste

1 cup dark chocolate chips

MAKE IT

1. Preheat oven to 350°F. Line a baking sheet with parchment paper.

2. Place almond flour, cocoa powder, and salt in a medium bowl and stir to combine.

3. Fold in coconut oil, maple syrup, and peppermint extract until evenly incorporated.

4. Allow batter to rest for 10 minutes in the refrigerator.

5. Roll 1 tablespoon of cookie batter between palms of hands to form a ball and place on baking sheet. Press to flatten into approximately a ⅛-inch-thick disc.

6. Bake for 10 minutes then cool a few minutes on the baking sheet before removing to a wire rack.

7. Melt half the chocolate chips in a double boiler. Take off heat and fold in remainder of chocolate to temper the mixture.

8. Dip cookies in chocolate and place them back on the parchment-lined baking sheet. Or you can drizzle chocolate on top of cookies.

9. Refrigerate cookies for 15 minutes to set chocolate coating.

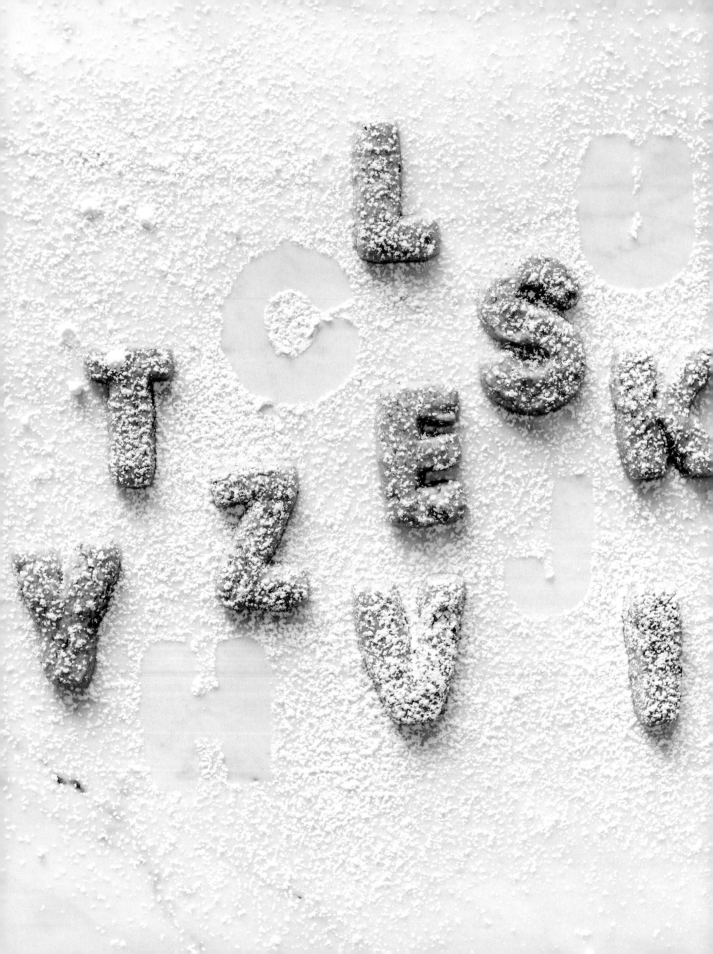

Ice Box Maple Cookies

MAKES 24 COOKIES

Maple sugar makes a great white sugar substitute
because it has the same sweetness level and a very similar fine texture.
It also is lower on the glycemic index in comparison to white sugar,
which means it raises blood sugar more slowly than the regular sweet stuff.

GATHER

1   stick (½ cup) unsalted butter, softened

¼   cup maple sugar

     Pinch of sea salt

1   teaspoon vanilla extract

1   cup spelt flour

½   cup pecans, finely chopped

MAKE IT

1. Preheat oven to 350°F and line 2 baking sheets with parchment paper.

2. Add butter and maple sugar to a bowl and use a hand mixer to whisk for 2–3 minutes, or until creamed.

3. Add salt and vanilla extract and stir until combined.

4. Add in the flour in stages, whisking with hand mixer until incorporated.

5. Fold in pecans then place batter in freezer for 5–10 minutes.

6. Using a rolling pin, roll out cookie dough into a ¼-inch thickness on 1 baking sheet. Place baking sheet into freezer so dough stiffens.

7. Cut out desired shapes using cookie cutters of choice, arranging on the other baking sheet.

8. Bake cookies for 10–12 minutes, or until lightly golden.

Flourless Spiced Gingerbread Cookies

MAKES 24 (1-INCH) COOKIES

Here's a gluten-free cookie that actually tastes better without the gluten. Adding real ground ginger into this cookie not only helps with flavor but it helps with digestion and blood sugar levels as well.

GATHER

1½ cups almond flour

¼ cup tapioca starch (arrowroot), more to dust

1 tablespoon ground ginger

Pinch of sea salt

2 tablespoons refined coconut oil

¼ cup maple syrup

1 tablespoon molasses

MAKE IT

1. Preheat oven to 350°F and line 2 baking sheets with parchment paper.

2. In a large bowl, add almond flour, tapioca starch, ground ginger, and salt, stirring to combine.

3. Incorporate in the coconut oil, maple syrup, and molasses until dough forms.

4. Place dough in freezer for 15 minutes, and using a rolling pin, roll out on 1 baking sheet into approximately ¼-inch thickness using additional tapioca starch to manage any sticking.

5. Place baking sheet in freezer for 5 minutes so dough stiffens.

6. Cut out shapes using desired cookie cutters, and place on other baking sheet.

8. Bake for 10–12 minutes.

9. Cool cookies, and drizzle with Nutmeg-Infused Icing, if using.

Nutmeg-Infused Icing

MAKES ¼ CUP

GATHER

½ cup organic confectioners' sugar

¼ teaspoon ground nutmeg

Pinch of sea salt

1½ teaspoons agave syrup

1½ teaspoons almond milk

MAKE IT

1. Add confectioners' sugar, nutmeg, and salt to a small bowl and stir to combine.

2. Fold in agave syrup and almond milk to form icing.

3. Allow mixture to rest for 5 minutes then drizzle on cookies

Chewy Cauliflower— Black Sesame Cookies

MAKES APPROXIMATELY 24 COOKIES

Yes, cauliflower. This is no typo. Cauliflower is nutrient dense in vitamin C and K and has practically no calories. It's also a blank canvas, meaning it can take on the flavor of whatever you're cooking—or in this case—-baking. A few tips: The cauliflower has to be cooked to tender and completely blended for a cookie that holds together. And roasting the black sesame seeds will bring out the flavor.

GATHER

2   cups small cauliflower florets (approximately 6 ounces)

1   (14-ounce) can coconut milk

3/4   cup maple syrup

2   teaspoons vanilla extract

Pinch of sea salt

1/2   cup black sesame seeds

2   cups whole-wheat flour

2   teaspoons baking powder

MAKE IT

1. Preheat oven to 350°F, and line 2 baking sheets with parchment paper.

2. Place cauliflower, coconut milk, maple syrup, vanilla extract, and salt into a small pan. Bring to simmer, and cook for 10 minutes or until florets are tender.

3. Transfer mixture to wide container (will help cool quicker) and place in freezer to cool for 15 minutes. Note: It should still be warm.

4. Blend in blender until smooth.

5. Toast sesame seeds in a pan over medium heat for 2 minutes, stirring occasionally.

6. Cool seeds and then combine with whole-wheat flour and baking powder in medium bowl. Fold in cauliflower mixture to flour mixture.

7. Scoop 2 tablespoons cookie dough onto baking sheets and bake on center-most racks for 15 minutes, or until lightly firm to the touch.

8. Transfer to wire racks to cool. Store in airtight container for 3–5 days.

Parsnip—Brown Butter Sugar Cookies

MAKES 24 COOKIES

So, you might be asking: why parsnips? Sure, it has fiber, protein, and vitamins. But it's also a fantastic add-in to help reduce the amount of butter you need in a recipe. Cooked parsnips do a beautiful job in emulsifying the ingredients, so you use less butter. Less butter means more cookies for you to eat. Got it?

GATHER

- 1 medium parsnip
- 1 stick ($\frac{1}{2}$ cup) unsalted butter
- 1 cup coconut sugar
- 2 teaspoons vanilla extract
- 1 organic egg
- 2 teaspoons baking powder
- 1$\frac{1}{2}$ cups whole-wheat flour
- $\frac{1}{2}$ teaspoon flaky sea salt

MAKE IT

1. Preheat oven to 350°F, and line 2 baking sheets with parchment paper.

2. Peel and dice parsnip (approximately 1$\frac{3}{4}$ cups), and place in small pot. Cover with cold water, bring to boil, and cook for 10 minutes, or until tender. Drain, spread onto a plate and cool in freezer for 10 minutes.

3. Place butter into a pan and cook over medium heat for 3 minutes or until golden. Transfer into bowl and place in freezer for 10 minutes to cool.

4. Cream together cooled butter, cooled parsnip, and coconut sugar for 2 minutes using a stand or electric hand mixer.

5. Add vanilla extract and egg and continue to beat for additional minute, scraping down edges as needed. Whisk baking powder into flour and fold into wet mixture.

6. Scoop 1-ounce (2 tablespoons) rounds onto baking sheet, placing 12 cookies per tray approximately 2 inches apart. Use a fork to gently flatten and sprinkle with sea salt. Bake on center-most racks for 16–18 minutes, or until lightly golden.

7. Transfer to wire rack to cool. Store in airtight container for 3–5 days.

Beet, Aquafaba, and Rose Macarons

MAKES 18 COOKIES (36 HALVES)

Listen, this won't be a recipe that's an everyday staple in your baking repertoire.
But it's not difficult either. It just takes a few extra steps to make truly one of the most
decadent cookies you've ever made at home. And in case you're wondering what aquafaba is,
it's basically the milky brine in a can of chickpeas. So save it and give these a whirl!

GATHER

- $3/4$ cup no-salt-added aquafaba (1 can of chickpeas)
- 1 small beet
- $3/4$ cup organic cane sugar, sifted and divided
- $3/4$ cup almond flour, sifted
- $1/2$ teaspoon cream of tartar
- $1/4$ teaspoon rose water, or to taste
- $1/2$ cup seedless raspberry jam

MAKE IT

1. Preheat oven to 275°F (no fan), and line 2 baking sheets with parchment paper.

2. Place aquafaba in small pot and reduce for 10 minutes over medium heat, or until reduced to $1/3$ cup.

3. Cool mixture completely in freezer for 15 minutes.

4. Grate beet and press through a strainer to extract juice into a bowl.

5. Sift $1/4$ cup sugar and almond flour into a medium bowl and whisk to combine; set aside.

6. Use stand or electric hand mixer to beat the cooled chickpea reduction on high speed. Sift in the cream of tartar after 30 seconds.

7. Add remaining sugar by the tablespoon after mixture starts to foam.

8. Beat on high for 3–5 minutes, or until stiff glossy peaks form.

9. Gently fold in flour mixture into whipped mixture. Stir in beet juice (approximately 2 tablespoons) and rosewater.

10. Use a small metal spoon to spoon 2-inch mounds of batter onto baking sheets.

11. Bake on center rack for 25–30 minutes, or until slightly firm to the touch. Allow to cool completely before transferring onto wire rack. Note: If transferred when still hot, they will stick to the parchment paper.

12. Add 1 teaspoon jam between 2 macarons, repeating for remainder of cookies.

13. Enjoy or place in refrigerator to soften for a few hours before consuming.

Gluten-Free Zucchini Muesli Cookies

MAKES 18 COOKIES

Healthy? Check. Zero gluten? Yep. Could you grab these and eat them for breakfast? You absolutely freaking could. These are the most guilt-free cookies in the bunch. By the way, zucchini is added for two reasons: to slip in some veg and keep these cookies moist and chewy.

GATHER

1 medium zucchini

½ cup refined coconut oil

1 cup gluten-free muesli (substitute granola for the muesli for a sweeter finish)

¾ cup coconut sugar

¼ cup ground flax seeds

1 cup gluten-free flour mix (I like Bob's Red Mill)

1 teaspoon baking powder

Pinch of sea salt

MAKE IT

1. Preheat oven to 350°F, and line 2 baking sheets with parchment paper.

2. Shred zucchini into a medium bowl (approximately $1\,1/2$ cups).

3. Melt coconut oil and stir into zucchini.

4. In a separate bowl, stir together muesli, coconut sugar, ground flax, flour mix, baking powder, and salt; fold into zucchini mixture.

5. Allow mixture to rest for 5 minutes to activate flax.

6. Using a 2-tablespoon scoop, drop cookies onto baking sheets, leaving 2 inches of space in between as cookies will spread. Bake on center-most racks for 15–18 minutes, or until golden and firm to the touch.

7. Cool on wire rack. Cookies can be stored in an airtight container for 3–5 days.

Vegetable Juice Fortune-Shaped Cookies

MAKES 20 COOKIES

This could easily enter Martha Stewart recipe territory (as in, who is crazy enough to make something you get for **free** in Chinese takeout?), but it just looks like it's a Martha-only recipe, I swear. You'd only go into Martha-land if you made custom paper fortunes embossed with gold leaf to slip into each of your homemade fortune cookies. So, don't . . . .

GATHER

- ¾ cup no-salt-added aquafaba (1 can of chickpeas)
- ½ teaspoon cream of tartar
- ½ cup organic cane sugar
- ¾ cup whole-wheat flour
- 3 tablespoons refined coconut oil, melted
- 1 teaspoon vanilla extract
- 3 tablespoons vegetable juice (carrot, beet, kale, or juice of choice)

MAKE IT

1. Preheat oven to 275°F and place an ovenproof rack on a baking sheet.

2. Place aquafaba in small pan and reduce for about 5 minutes, or by half. Cool completely in freezer for 15 minutes.

3. Add cream of tartar to aquafaba using a stand or electric hand mixer and whip on high speed for 2 minutes or until fluffy. Add sugar while continuing to beat. Gently sift and fold flour into aquafaba mixture.

4. Add coconut oil to mixture along with vanilla extract and vegetable juice. Or split batter into 3 bowls and add 1 tablespoon of juice to each bowl, using different juices. Add a few tablespoons of water to form a thin pancake batter consistency.

5. Warm nonstick pan over low heat. Working in batches, pour 1 tablespoon of batter into a thin 3-inch round. Cook for 4–5 minutes and gently fold in half using a small flexible spatula. Use spatula to curve cookie into a fortune shape by pushing the edges inward. Transfer onto rack and repeat process with remaining batter.

6. Cookies are ready to eat, or can be baked for 20–25 minutes to attain a crisper texture.

Spinach—Peppermint Crème Whoopie Pies

MAKES 7 ASSEMBLED WHOOPIE PIES

I'm not going to lie and tell you these are the best looking whoopie pies you've ever seen. Actually, the green frosting kind reminds me of really creamy, slightly thinned out guacamole. They are, however, delicious. A great recipe to make for kids who love gross looking but delicious treats. But if the green filling is throwing you off, just omit the spinach.

GATHER

- 3 cups baby spinach
- 1 cup cashews
- $1/2$ teaspoon peppermint extract, or to taste
- 1 cup agave nectar, divided

  Pinch of sea salt
- $1/2$ cup cocoa powder
- $1^1/2$ cups oat flour
- 2 tablespoons ground flax seeds
- $1^1/2$ teaspoons baking powder
- 1 (14-ounce) can coconut milk

MAKE IT

1. Preheat oven to 350°F, and line 2 baking sheets with parchment paper.

2. Fill medium pot halfway with water and bring to a boil. Add spinach and cashews and cook for 15 seconds or until spinach is wilted. Drain into a colander positioned in a sink and rinse with cold water until cool.

3. Place spinach and cashews in blender, along with peppermint extract, $1/2$ cup of agave nectar and salt and process until smooth. Chill in refrigerator until ready to use.

4. Whisk together cocoa powder, oat flour, ground flax seeds, and baking powder in a medium bowl.

5. Stir in remaining agave nectar and coconut milk until batter forms.

6. Spoon $1/4$ cup mounds onto baking sheets, using a spoon to spread in approximate 3-inch circles, leaving approximately 2 inches in between each mound.

7. Bake for 18 minutes, or until cookies spring back to the touch. Cool.

8. Spread 2 heaping tablespoons of spinach peppermint crème onto the flat side of 1 cookie and use additional cookie to create the whoopie pie. Repeat with remainder of cookies and crème.

9. Store refrigerated in airtight container for 3–5 days.

Root Vegetable Fun-fetti Cookies

MAKES 24 COOKIES

There was some controversy over a word in this recipe. And that word is "optional." I objected, because how can you make a "fun-fetti" cookie if you don't have colorful sprinkles on top? So I must insist: if you omit the sprinkles, just tell folks you made a "root vegetable cookie." That said, it's a keeper and the candied ginger root is the hero ingredient that adds a lively sweetness to these cookies.

GATHER

- 3 medium multi-colored carrots
- ½ cup candied ginger root
- ¾ cup coconut sugar
- 1½ cups whole-wheat flour
- 2 tablespoons ground flax seeds
- 1½ teaspoons baking powder
- 2 cans coconut cream (approximately 1½ cups)
- ¾ cup natural sprinkles (optional)

MAKE

1. Preheat oven to 350°F, and line 2 baking sheets with parchment paper.

2. Peel and grate carrots (approximately 1¾ cups total).

3. Chop candied ginger and set aside.

4. Whisk together coconut sugar, flour, flax seeds, and baking powder in a medium bowl.

5. Fold in carrot mixture, chopped candied ginger, and coconut cream until batter forms. Do not over mix.

6. Scoop batter using 1-ounce scoop onto baking sheets, leaving 2-inches between each cookie.

7. If a more colorful cookie is desired, sprinkle each cookie with sprinkles, pressing the sprinkles gently into the batter.

8. Bake on center-most racks for 18–20 minutes, or until lightly golden and slightly firm to the touch.

Paleo Sweet Potato— Cinnamon Crunch Cookies

MAKES APPROXIMATELY 30 COOKIES

If you think doing a Paleo diet means desserts are a thing of the past, think again. I love these cookies because they don't taste **healthy**. Instead, they are sweet, spicy, moist, and hit the spot when you just want a little something sweet. And, yes, you can have more than just one.

GATHER

1½ cups pecans, divided

1 medium sweet potato

1 can coconut cream (approximately ⅔ cup)

8 Medjool dates, pitted

4 teaspoons ground cinnamon

2 cups almond flour

1 teaspoon baking powder

¼ teaspoon sea salt

MAKE IT

1. Preheat oven to 350°F, and line 2 baking sheets with parchment paper.

2. Toast 1 cup of pecans in oven for 5 minutes, reserving remaining half cup for garnish. Cool and chop coarsely.

3. Peel and dice sweet potato (approximately 2 cups). Place in small pot, cover with water, bring to a boil, and cook for 10 minutes, or until tender.

4. Drain and transfer to a blender, along with coconut cream. Add dates along with cinnamon and blend until smooth.

5. In a medium bowl, stir together almond flour, chopped pecans, baking powder, and salt.

6. Stir in wet mixture into almond flour mixture.

7. Scoop cookies using 1-ounce scoop onto baking sheets. Top with remaining pecans by pressing 1 gently atop each cookie and bake on center-most racks for 18–20 minutes.

8. Transfer onto wire rack to cool, and store in airtight container for 3–5 days.

Black Cocoa "Oreos" with Cauliflower Crème

MAKES 28 SANDWICH COOKIES

Yes, we came up a healthy version of the American classic Oreo. And, yes, it only took us five years to figure it out. You see, cauliflower turns out to be the hero veg to use for the crème; it has just enough of a subtle cultured flavor akin to cream cheese.

GATHER

1½ cups cauliflower florets

1 cup cashews

1¾ cups organic cane sugar, divided

⅛ teaspoon sea salt

¾ cup black cocoa powder

1 cup whole-wheat flour

1 teaspoon baking powder

2 tablespoons ground flax seeds

1 (14-ounce) can coconut milk

MAKE IT

1. Preheat oven to 350°F, and line 2 baking sheets with parchment paper.

2. Place cauliflower florets and cashews into a small pot and cover with water.

3. Bring to a boil and cook for 5 minutes or until tender.

4. Drain and blend cauliflower and cashews in blender along with 1 cup sugar and salt, processing until smooth. Cool completely in refrigerator.

5. Whisk together remaining sugar, cocoa powder, flour, baking powder, and ground flax in a medium bowl.

6. Fold in coconut milk.

7. Using a 1-tablespoon measure, scoop batter onto baking sheets and use a spoon to flatten into approximate 1-inch rounds. Cookies will spread, so leave 1–2 inches between rounds.

8. Bake on center-most oven racks for 16–18 minutes or until firm to the touch and transfer onto a wire rack.

9. Reduce oven heat to 250°F and place rack of cookies back onto baking tray and dry out for at least 25 minutes, or longer if crispier cookies are desired. Cool completely.

10. Before serving, spread 1 tablespoon of crème onto half the cookies and use remainder of the cookies to press into a sandwich, positioning flat side of sandwiching cookie upward.

Chewy Chocolate-Avocado Protein Cookies

MAKES APPROXIMATELY 21 COOKIES

Are you on the collagen bandwagon? Collagen is a flavorless and odorless high-protein amino acid that your body needs for a healthy gut, flexible joints, strong muscles, and to even look younger with less wrinkles. I put a scoop of collagen in my coffee every morning, but it can also be added to things you bake. In this case, the collagen is more than a booster, it also helps bind the batter. And the avocado has 3 purposes: sweetness, fat, and moisture to help emulsify everything together.

GATHER

1	ripe avocado
¾	cup agave nectar
2	teaspoons vanilla extract
¼	cup unflavored collagen powder
1	cup quinoa flour
1	teaspoon baking powder
1	cup dark chocolate chips
½	teaspoon flaky sea salt

MAKE IT

1. Preheat oven to 350°F, and line 2 baking sheets with parchment paper.

2. Process avocado, agave nectar, and vanilla extract in food processor or blender until smooth.

3. In a medium bowl, whisk together collagen powder, quinoa flour, and baking powder.

4. Fold in puréed avocado mixture and chocolate chips.

5. Use a 1-ounce scoop to transfer cookies onto baking sheets.

6. Bake on center-most racks for 18–20 minutes or until golden and lightly firm to the touch.

7. Transfer to wire rack to cool; store in airtight container for 3–5 days.

Avocado Boston Cream Pie Cookies

MAKES 18 COOKIES

If you learn one thing from this chapter, it's this: Regular 'ole cocoa powder mixed
with agave syrup creates an instant and insanely delicious chocolate sauce.
And that sauce goes even better on these Boston cream pie cookies. BTW, we add
turmeric to the custard to give it a nutritional boost and a custard-like glow.

GATHER

1 ripe avocado

1¾ cups agave syrup, divided

1 tablespoon vanilla extract, divided

1½ cups gluten-free flour mix (I like Bob's Red Mill)

1½ teaspoons baking powder

2 tablespoons organic cornstarch

1 cup coconut milk

Pinch of ground turmeric

½ cup cocoa powder

MAKE IT

1. Preheat oven to 350°F, and line 2 baking sheets with parchment paper.

2. Purée avocado, ¾ cup agave syrup, and 1 teaspoon vanilla extract in food processor or blender.

3. Whisk together flour mix and baking powder in a medium bowl. Fold in avocado mixture.

4. Use a 1-ounce scoop to transfer cookies onto baking sheets.

5. Bake on center-most racks for 16–18 minutes or until golden and lightly firm to the touch and transfer to wire rack to cool.

6. Dissolve cornstarch in a small bowl with a few tablespoons of water, add to small pan along with coconut milk, ½ cup agave syrup, and remaining vanilla extract and bring to a simmer.

7. Whisk for 2–5 minutes on a medium heat or until mixture thickens. Stir in turmeric and take off heat to cool.

8. Add remaining agave syrup and cocoa powder to a small pan. Stir on low heat until cocoa powder dissolves.

9. Place 1 tablespoon of custard on each cookie and top with chocolate spread. Note: For neater appearance, place chocolate mixture into piping bag and pipe onto each cookie.

Matcha-Dusted Gluten-Free Almond Biscotti

MAKES 12 BISCOTTI

If you'd like to make this biscotti totally plant based, just replace the eggs with 2 tablespoons of ground chia or flax seeds. These are excellent with a cup of coffee.

GATHER

1 teaspoon baking powder

1½ cups almond flour

1 cup sorghum flour

⅓ cup refined coconut oil

⅓ cup maple syrup

1 organic egg

GARNISH

½ cup slivered almonds, more for garnish

½ cup dark chocolate chips

2 teaspoons matcha powder

MAKE IT

1. Preheat oven to 350°F and line a baking sheet with parchment paper.

2. Sift together baking powder, almond flour, and sorghum flour in a bowl. Stir to combine.

3. Warm coconut oil briefly until melted. Remove from heat and stir in maple syrup and beat in egg.

4. Pour oil mixture into flour mixture, folding until combined. Mixture will be sticky.

5. Roll dough in almonds and form a log that measures approximately 12 x 3 inches long. Place on center of baking sheet and bake for 25 minutes or until golden.

6. Cool for a few minutes and slice into 1-inch slices and place slices back on wire rack.

7. Place wire rack on top of baking sheet and bake for additional 10–15 minutes.

8. Melt ¼ cup chocolate chips over double boiler. Remove from heat and stir in remaining chocolate to temper mixture.

9. Spread chocolate mixture on top half of biscotti and dust with matcha powder. Top with extra almonds.

CHILL OUT

No, we're not talking about Elsa here. But she'd probably like these chilled treats.

There are two reasons why I love a chilled or frozen dessert. First, you can have an ample supply stashed away and enjoy it in a moment's notice if you're hankering for something sweet. And when it's sweltering hot outside or you've just eaten a meal that's warmed up the body, it can be a nice, cooling contrast to bite, lick, or chomp on something cold.

You night notice this isn't a chapter about making homemade ice creams. There are very few of those kinds of recipes, and here's why: I don't own an ice cream maker, and I bet many of you don't either. I'm not a fan of buying a bulky machine for the sake of making a recipe. My mind always goes to the TV show "Hoarders" and the dilemma of where on earth I'm going to store that clunker of a machine? Somewhere Marie Kondo is nodding her head in agreement because while that ice cream brings me joy, does that machine? Not so much.

Instead, I focused on use of the refrigerator and freezer to be that one step that does exactly that: chills or freezes. That's it. Whether it's pops, parfaits, sherbet, shakes, or frozen tarts, there are plenty of cool (see what I did here?) options you're gonna love.

Creamsicle Cashew "Cheesecake"

MAKES 1 (8-INCH) CAKE

I cringe when someone uses air-quote fingers to describe a recipe. But in this case, we use quotes because while it looks and tastes like a yummy cheesecake, it's actually totally raw, gluten-free, and dairy-free. You can make it large in a springform pan or just use small cups to make individual-size ones. And change up the flavors, too; instead of orange marmalade, try frozen blueberries, caramel, or strawberry.

GATHER

FOR THE CRUST

1   cup dates, pitted

1   cup pecans, lightly toasted

     Pinch of sea salt

FOR THE SWIRL

¼   cup orange marmalade

2 to 4 tablespoons filtered water

FOR THE FILLING

2   cups cashews, soaked and drained

½   cup filtered water

½   cup maple syrup

½   cup coconut oil

1   lemon, juiced

½   tablespoon vanilla extract

1   tablespoon orange extract

MAKE IT

1. Pulse the dates, pecans, and salt in a food processor until slightly sticky, but still retains some texture. Press into an 8-inch springform pan and place in freezer until ready to fill.

2. In a small saucepan, warm marmalade and water. Use an immersion blender to smooth. Pass through strainer.

3. In a high-speed blender, process the cashews, water, maple syrup, coconut oil, lemon juice, and extracts until mixture is very smooth.

4. Pour "cheesecake" batter into chilled springform pan and add random spoonfuls of marmalade mixture on surface. Use a skewer to drag mixture, to create a marbled effect. Place in freezer to firm up for 1–2 hours. Keep frozen and slice before serving.

Raspberry Tiramisu Parfait

MAKES 4 INDIVIDUAL SERVINGS

Here's a restaurant-quality crowd pleaser that
literally takes less than 15 minutes to make. Think of it as our take
on Sandra Lee's semi-homemade, sans the Cool Whip.

GATHER

16 lady fingers (or amaretti cookies), divided

1 cup strong-brewed coffee

½ cup chocolate syrup

2 cups plain yogurt

½ cup raspberry jam

1 pint fresh raspberries

2 tablespoons cocoa powder

MAKE IT

1. Dip 8 lady fingers in coffee for 2–3 seconds, or until saturated, but not disintegrating to the touch.

2. Place 2 soaked lady fingers in a glass, or clear bowl for an individual serving, repeating in 3 additional vessels. Drizzle each serving with 1 tablespoon of chocolate syrup.

3. Add $1/4$ cup of plain yogurt on top of chocolate syrup, followed by 1 tablespoon of raspberry jam, a few raspberries, and a dusting of cocoa powder. Repeat for each additional vessel.

4. Add second layer of each ingredient, using the same amounts and suggested order.

5. Refrigerate parfaits for at least 10 minutes before serving.

Frozen Winter-Citrus Sherbet

MAKES 4 SERVINGS

How lushy you want to be determines how slushy this winter citrus sherbet can become. While this recipe calls for a mere tablespoon of vodka, adding more can turn this frozen treat into a summery cocktail.

GATHER

1   tablespoon lemon zest

5   lemons, juiced

¾   cup agave nectar

3   cups coconut milk

1   teaspoon lemon extract

1   tablespoon vodka

     Pinch of sea salt

MAKE IT

1. Combine lemon zest, lemon juice, agave, coconut milk, lemon extract, vodka, and salt in a blender.

2. Blend until smooth. Season mixture to taste (should taste sweet).

3. Pour into a shallow baking dish and freeze; stirring every 20–30 minutes until totally frozen.

4. Transfer to freezer for 2–3 hours, to allow sherbet to harden before serving.

Vegan Apple-Hibiscus Jelly-O Gelatin

MAKES 4 SERVINGS

The sweetness of the apples and tartness of the hibiscus pair effortlessly, delivering both an aesthetic and sensory-pleasing treat. Use as an innovative top layer of a cake or torte, applying the warm gelatin when the confectionery is completely cool, and placing in the refrigerator to set.

This is also good for you. Hibiscus is not only vibrant in color, but shines when it comes to antioxidant levels and vitamin C. Apple juice can help you reduce inflammation and gain glowing skin.

GATHER

2   cups apple juice

2   tablespoons hibiscus tea leaves

2   tablespoons agave nectar (optional)

     Pinch of sea salt

3   tablespoons agar flakes

MAKE IT

1. Add juice and tea to a small pan and bring to a simmer.

2. Turn off heat and allow mixture to steep for 5 minutes.

3. Strain and discard tea leaves.

4. Add agave nectar, if using, along with salt and agar flakes and bring mixture back to a simmer.

5. Cook for 5 minutes, or until agar flakes have completely dissolved.

6. Pour mixture into desired container and chill in refrigerator for 30 minutes, or until firm.

Vegan Pineapple-Turmeric Jelly-O Gelatin

MAKES 4 SERVINGS

This luminous, golden gelatin is not only hydrating, but it is also full of fiber and has anti-inflammatory properties. After you use your favorite cookie cutter to cut pineapple shapes to suspend, simply blend or juice the remaining scraps to use as the juice for this recipe. This is a digestion powerhouse because pineapple contains bromelain, an enzyme that aids in the digestion of protein, and also helps maintain a healthy gut flora.

GATHER

1 small pineapple

2 cups pineapple juice

1 teaspoon turmeric powder

2 tablespoons agave nectar (optional)

Pinch of sea salt

3 tablespoons agar flakes

MAKE IT

1. Peel and cut the pineapple into $1/4$-inch slices. Use a small round cookie cutter, to cut out rounds, avoiding the core.

2. Add pineapple juice, turmeric powder, agave nectar, if using, and salt to a small pan and bring to a simmer.

3. Add agar flakes and cook over a low heat for 5 minutes, or until agar flakes have completely dissolved.

4. Pour mixture into desired container and top with pineapple rounds.

5. Chill for 30 minutes, or until firm.

Vegan Coconut-Chia Jelly-O Gelatin

MAKES 4 SERVINGS

This white, velvety gelatin is reminiscent of a tropical island vacation in a glass. When in a pinch, try omitting the seeds, and blending up the set gelatin in a food processor for a fast, more natural frosting. I chose coconut water because it provides essential electrolytes, boosting hydration and helping with proper muscle and nerve function, and it adds a nice flavor profile.

GATHER

1½ cups coconut water

½ cup coconut milk

½ teaspoon coconut extract

2 tablespoons agave nectar (optional)

Pinch of sea salt

3 tablespoons agar flakes

1 tablespoon chia seeds

MAKE IT

1. Add coconut water, coconut milk, coconut extract, agave nectar, and salt to a small pan and bring to a simmer.

2. Add agar flakes and cook over a low heat for 5 minutes, or until agar flakes have completely dissolved.

3. Stir in chia seeds, and allow mixture to sit for 1 minute.

4. Pour coconut chia mixture into desired container.

5. Chill in refrigerator for 30 minutes, or until firm.

Vegan Blackberry-Jasmine Jelly-O Gelatin

MAKES 4 SERVINGS

This purple-hued treat accentuates the floral notes from the jasmine and brims with ripe blackberries to give you an energy boost any time of day. Use any berry you have on hand or try different frozen berry varieties like strawberry or wild blueberry. You can swap out the jasmine tea leaves for almost any other herbal tea, too.

GATHER

2   cups water

¾   cup frozen blackberries

1   tablespoon jasmine tea leaves

¼   cup agave nectar (optional)

     Pinch of sea salt

3   tablespoons agar flakes

2   tablespoons lemon juice

⅓   cup blackberries, cut in half lengthwise

MAKE IT

1. Add water, frozen blackberries, and tea leaves to a small pan and bring to a simmer.

2. Turn off heat and allow mixture to steep for 5 minutes.

3. Strain, and discard tea leaves and blackberries.

4. Add agave nectar, if using, along with salt and agar flakes; bring mixture back to a simmer.

5. Cook for 5 minutes, or until agar flakes have completely dissolved.

6. Stir in lemon juice.

7. Pour mixture into desired container and garnish with cut blackberries.

8. Chill in refrigerator for 30 minutes, or until firm.

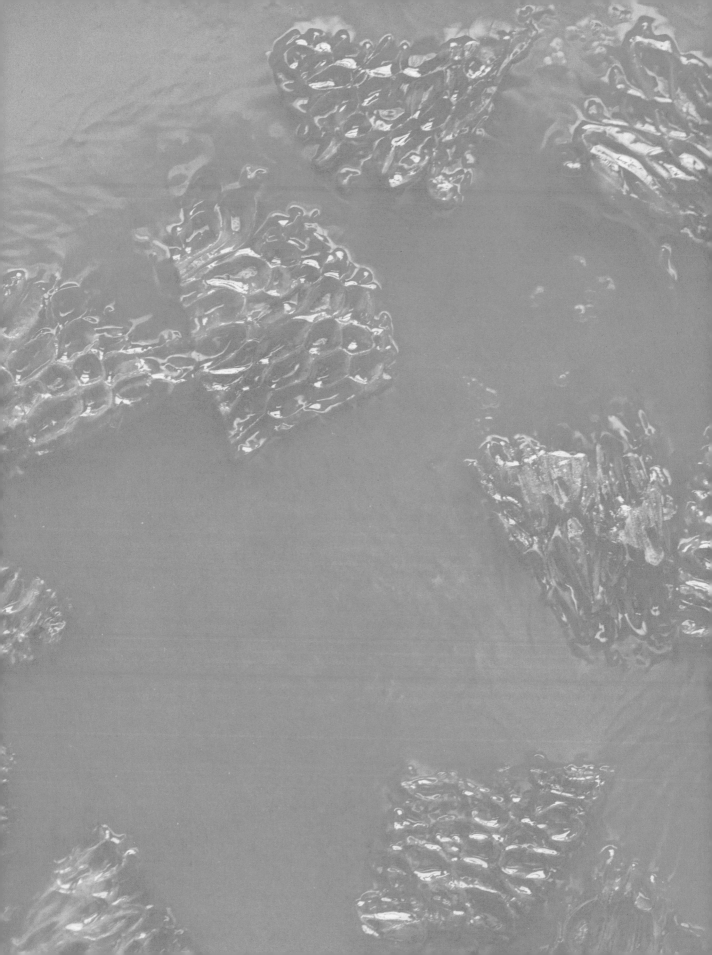

Vegetarian Grapefruit-Honey Jelly-O Gelatin

MAKES 4 SERVINGS

Yes, vegetarian and not vegan. Because the use of honey makes it not exactly 100% plant based. If you want to vegan-ize this, just swap out the honey for agave or another sweetener. The sweet, tart, and citrus flavors come to life in a melodious pink-hued gelatin, making this winning combination both chic and irresistible. Create a "creamsicle" flavor by substituting the grapefruit with oranges and adding a dash of vanilla extract.

GATHER

2 cups pink grapefruit juice

3 tablespoons honey

Pinch of sea salt

3 tablespoons agar flakes

1 small pink grapefruit

MAKE IT

1. Add grapefruit juice, honey, and salt to a small pan and bring to a simmer.

2. Add agar flakes and cook over a low heat for 5 minutes, or until agar flakes have completely dissolved.

3. Using a sharp knife, trim the skin and pith off the grapefruit, and slice the flesh into $1/4$-inch slices. Cut slices into quarters to create smaller segments.

4. Pour mixture into desired container and top with grapefruit.

5. Chill for 30 minutes, or until firm.

Raspberry-Lemon Swirl Frozen "Cheesecake" Pops

MAKES 18 POPS

I love this plant-based recipe because it satisfies a sweet tooth in small doses with the use of lollipop sticks. And because it's a dairy-free mixture, it also melts more slowly, making it an ideal treat to bring outdoors during the hot summer months.

GATHER

FOR THE RASPBERRY SWIRL

1	cup frozen raspberries
1/4	cup maple syrup

FOR THE "CHEESECAKE" MIXTURE

2	cups cashews, soaked
1/2	cup coconut oil, melted
1/2	cup maple syrup
1	lemon, zested and juiced
1/2	cup filtered water
1	teaspoon vanilla extract
1	teaspoon lemon extract
	Pinch of sea salt
18	lollipop sticks

MAKE IT

1. Add the raspberries and maple syrup to a small saucepan and bring to a simmer. Stir occasionally, and cook on low heat for approximately 10 minutes, or until mixture reduces down to 1/2 cup in volume.

2. Break up any remaining large pieces of raspberries. Allow mixture to cool to room temperature.

3. Drain and rinse the soaked cashews, and place in a high-speed blender along with the melted coconut oil, maple syrup, lemon zest, lemon juice, water, vanilla extract, lemon extract, and salt.

4. Blend ingredients for 1 minute, or until creamy. Pour "cheesecake" batter into an 8 x 8-inch dish and place dollops of the raspberry mixture on top, using a skewer to swirl into the batter. Repeat until all the raspberry mixture is used up.

5. Allow batter to firm for approximately 1 hour in the freezer. Use a 1-ounce ice cream scoop to shape the mixture into spheres. Insert lollipop sticks and return to the freezer for an additional 10 minutes. Keep frozen until ready to serve.

Turmeric and Maple Golden Gelato

MAKES 4 SERVINGS

This recipe was inspired by a trip we took up north to visit maple growers in Canada.
We spent a lot of time in sugar shacks, and thought if we just used pure, whole ingredients,
what could a delicious frozen treat look like? This is what we came up with.
It's on the heavier side, so a little taste goes a long way.

GATHER

3	cups organic milk
1	cup organic heavy cream
½	cup maple syrup
2	teaspoons turmeric powder
1	tablespoon vanilla extract
1	vanilla bean, scraped
	Pinch of sea salt
½	cup maple sugar
6	large egg yolks

MAKE IT

1. In a small pot, slightly warm the milk, cream, maple syrup, turmeric powder, vanilla extract, scraped vanilla bean, and salt. Set up a double boiler, using a separate pot.

2. In a medium bowl, whisk together the maple sugar and egg yolks for 3 minutes, or until light and fluffy.

3. Place bowl with egg mixture over double boiler and slowly stream in lightly warm milk mixture, stirring vigorously until mixture thickens.

4. Pour into a shallow baking dish and freeze, stirring every 20–30 minutes until frozen. Transfer to freezer in an airtight container.

Maca Honeycomb Frozen Yogurt

MAKES 4 SERVINGS

Some believe eating maca—a Peruvian ginseng—can help stimulate the libido in both men and women. Whether or not it's true, it is a beneficial super-ingredient that helps boost energy and can boost your immune system. We add frozen grapes instead of ice so it can add natural sweetness without watering it down.

GATHER

1   cup organic Greek yogurt

1   tablespoon maca powder (I like the MegaFood brand)

3   cup green grapes, roughly chopped and frozen

TOPPINGS

¼   cup honeycomb, sliced

¼   cup sliced almonds

½   cup blackberries, cut in half lengthwise

MAKE IT

1. In a small bowl, stir together the yogurt with maca powder and allow to sit for a few minutes to rehydrate the powder.

2. Add frozen grapes, and yogurt mixture to a blender and purée until smooth.

3. Transfer to the freezer to firm for 30–60 minutes.

4. Scoop into serving dishes and garnish with sliced honeycomb, almonds, and blackberries.

Maca, Frozen Banana, and Toasted Coconut "Milkshake"

MAKES 1 (12-OUNCE) SERVING

This is a delicious milkshake that can easily be poured into a container and frozen to be made into a totally vegan ice cream. For caramel lovers, this one is a winner.

GATHER

2	teaspoons maca powder
1/3	cup pitted dates
1/3	cup filtered water
	Pinch of sea salt
2	frozen sliced bananas
1/2	cup thick coconut yogurt
1	vanilla bean, scraped

GARNISH

2	tablespoons large coconut flakes, toasted briefly in pan

MAKE IT

1. Add maca powder, dates, water, and salt to a blender and purée until smooth. Transfer this caramel mixture into a small bowl.

2. In the same blender (no need to rinse), combine the bananas (reserve a few pieces for garnish), coconut yogurt, and scraped vanilla bean and blend until smooth.

3. Fill a glass halfway with the "milkshake," drizzle in a generous spoonful of caramel, and fill the remainder of the glass.

4. Top "milkshake" with another drizzle of caramel, banana slices, and toasted coconut flakes.

Summer Peach and Avocado Swirl Popsicles

MAKES 10 POPSICLES

I love using avocados in desserts because it has a neutral flavor that takes on whatever you're mixing in with it. It also has a high level of good fats, which means the end result is both creamy and slow melting. What's not to love about a popsicle on a hot summer day that doesn't quickly melt away?

GATHER

3/4 cup cashews, soaked

1 (14-ounce) can coconut milk

1/4 cup agave syrup

Pinch of sea salt

1 (1/2-inch) piece ginger root, peeled

ADD-INS

1 ripe avocado

1 cup fresh or frozen peach slices

MAKE IT

1. Drain and rinse soaked cashews. Add to a blender along with coconut milk, agave syrup, salt, and ginger and blend until completely smooth.

2. Divide cashew mixture in half and blend one half separately with the avocado and the other half briefly with the peaches (small pieces should remain).

3. Fill popsicle molds about 3/4 of the way full with peach mixture.

4. Spoon the avocado mixture on top and use a popsicle stick to swirl it lightly into the peach batter.

5. Insert popsicle sticks and freeze for 1–2 hours, or until firm.

Avocado, Coconut, and Lime Sherbet

MAKES 1 PINT

Avocado is a delicious fruit to use for dairy-free treats because it has a
creamy consistency. The key is to use a very ripe avocado for this recipe;
anything slightly firm will result in a less creamy and more chunky sherbet.
You can also pour the mixture into popsicle molds to make pops, too!

GATHER

1   (14-ounce) can coconut milk, chilled

2   limes, zested and juiced

¼   cup agave nectar

    Pinch of sea salt

1   ripe avocado

GARNISH

¼   cup coconut flakes

1   lime, sliced

MAKE IT

1. Add coconut milk, lime zest (approximately 2 teaspoons), lime juice (approximately 4 teaspoons), agave, and salt to a blender.

2. Blend mixture until smooth.

3. Add avocado flesh, blending again just until combined.

4. Pour into a shallow baking dish and freeze, stirring every 20–30 minutes until frozen. Place in freezer for an additional hour to firm up.

5. Scoop sherbet and serve garnished with coconut flakes and lime slices.

Matcha-Gato: Matcha Shot with Churned Vanilla "Ice Cream"

MAKES 4 SERVINGS

The shot of matcha is optional. You can pour over caramel, homemade chocolate sauce, or just crumble up some cookies on top. And, yes, you can also just eat it plan as it is because this is a darn good dairy-free vanilla ice cream recipe.

GATHER

1 vanilla bean

1½ cups coconut cream

½ cup pitted dates

Pinch of sea salt

FOR THE MATCHA SHOT

4 teaspoons matcha powder

2 cups water

MAKE IT

1. Scrape vanilla bean and place seeds in blender along with coconut cream, dates, and salt.

2. Blend for 1 minute or until smooth. Pour into a shallow baking dish and freeze, stirring every 20–30 minutes until frozen. Transfer to freezer to solidify.

3. Add matcha powder and water into a bowl and use a matcha whisk to dissolve any lumps and create froth (alternatively place in blender and blend until smooth).

4. Scoop vanilla "ice cream" into 4 glasses or bowls and pour matcha on top of each. Serve right away.

Frozen Matcha Mousse Tart

SERVES 6 TO 8

If you don't have a 9-inch springform pan, an 8-inch one will work just fine, and so would a pie or cake pan. The only reason a springform pan is called for is that it ensures it's easy to get slices out of the pan. So, if you're gonna Instagram the hell out of this recipe, use that pan.

GATHER

FOR THE CRUST

1½ cups cashews, soaked in water for 2–8 hours and drained

2 tablespoons melted coconut oil

1 cup unsweetened shredded coconut

1 cup pitted dates

3 tablespoons unsweetened cocoa powder

FOR THE FILLING

1½ cups raw cashews soaked in water for 2–8 hours and drained

½ cup coconut cream

½ cup maple syrup

1 small avocado, peeled and pitted

1 tablespoon matcha tea

Pinch of sea salt

FOR THE TOPPING

Cocoa powder and matcha powder for dusting

¼ cup toasted unsweetened shredded coconut

MAKE IT

1. Grease a 9-inch springform pan.

2. Put the cashews for the crust in a food processor and pulse several times. Add the remaining crust ingredients and continue to pulse until a smooth dough forms. Using your fingers, press the dough into an even layer in the bottom of the prepared pan. Chill in the refrigerator while you prepare the filling.

3. Put the cashews for the filling in a food processor and run until finely ground. Add the remaining filling ingredients and continue to run until completely smooth (this may take a few minutes).

4. Pour the filling over the chilled crust. Cover and place in the freezer. Chill for 1 hour or until the center no longer jiggles.

5. Dust with matcha and cocoa powder, and then sprinkle with toasted coconut. Serve frozen.

Bullet-Proof Coffee Coconut Popsicles

MAKES 10 POPSICLES

It's energizing. It's creamy. It's cool. And it's something anyone on a low-carb diet can enjoy and not ruin their diet plan.

GATHER

- 3 (14-ounce) cans coconut milk
- Pinch of sea salt
- 6 cinnamon sticks
- 1 vanilla bean
- 2 tablespoons instant coffee
- 2 tablespoons collagen powder
- 1 unsweetened chocolate bar

MAKE IT

1. Add coconut milk, salt, and cinnamon sticks to medium saucepan. Scrape vanilla bean, and add seeds and pod to same pan.

2. Bring mixture to a simmer and cook on low heat for 15–20 minutes, or until mixture reduces by half (about 3 cups). Cool mixture for 15 minutes.

3. Remove and discard vanilla pod and cinnamon sticks.

4. Add $1/3$ of mixture into popsicle molds and place in freezer.

5. Stir instant coffee and collagen powder into remaining coconut milk until fully dissolved.

6. Add into molds and freeze for 4 hours or until completely frozen.

7. Remove popsicles and lay onto a parchment-lined tray. Return to freezer.

8. Simmer water in a pot and place a heatproof glass bowl on top. Break up the chocolate bar into pieces, add to the bowl and stir until completely melted. Use a spoon to drizzle chocolate on popsicles and return to freezer until ready to serve.

DOUGH BOY

I was in a very popular restaurant in Los Angeles where a lot of shiny, happy, pretty people were dining around me. I was also the only one with a bread basket on the table.

I don't know what it is, but people seem to think bread is akin to narcotics. You hear it all the time from folks who abstain from bread that it's more addictive than drugs. It's the reason you gain so much belly weight. It's just an unnecessary evil that should be banned from the dining table. But here I was, enjoying my bread basket with envious stares around me as if I was Brad Pitt holding an Oscar and handing out stacks of cash.

I get that baked treats are full of carbohydrates, and I suppose eating a lot of it turns into extra LBS around the waistline. But I also believe life is about moderation and not deprivation. Which is why I think it's worth making your cake and eating it, too. Stop staring and just dig in. These are all worth the carb-loaded calories . . . every . . . single . . . crumb.

Luscious Banana Cake

MAKES 1 CAKE OR 4 GENEROUS SLICES

The secret to this cake is the addition of tofu to the cream cheese frosting.
It adds a silkiness that makes a slice of this cake (almost) sinfully delicious.

GATHER

¼ cup butter

½ cup brown sugar

2 large eggs

1 cup whole-wheat flour

1 cup all-purpose white whole-wheat flour

¼ teaspoon salt

¼ teaspoon baking powder

½ cup milk

3 very ripe bananas, mashed

¾ teaspoon baking soda

1 teaspoon vanilla extract

FOR THE CREAM CHEESE FROSTING

¼ stick butter, softened

2 ounces silken tofu

6 ounces cream cheese, softened

½ cup confectioners' sugar

2 teaspoons vanilla extract

MAKE IT

1. Preheat oven to 350°F. Grease and flour a 9 x 13-inch baking pan.

2. In a large mixing bowl, cream butter and sugar. Add eggs and mix well.

3. In a separate bowl, sift flours, add salt and baking powder.

4. Add flour mixture and milk to the creamed butter mixture.

5. Fold in mashed bananas, baking soda, and vanilla extract. Pour into baking pan. Bake for 20–25 minutes.

FOR THE FROSTING

In a stand mixer, cream butter, silken tofu, cream cheese, sugar, and vanilla until smooth. Spread on cooled cake.

Flourless Toasted Almond Torte with Almond Gelato

MAKES 1 (10-INCH) TORTE; 4 CUPS GELATO

Eggs are a great source of iron and will help your skin glow, prevent dark circles around the eyes, and keep your scalp healthy. Making your own gelato is totally optional; a store-bought ice cream works perfectly fine with this recipe.

GATHER

FOR THE TORTE

1 tablespoon coconut oil

3 cups almond flour, plus extra for dusting

6 eggs

1 cup maple syrup

2 teaspoons almond extract

¼ cup slivered almonds

FOR THE GELATO

1½ cups whole milk

1½ cups heavy cream

⅔ cup maple sugar

5 egg yolks

1 teaspoon almond extract

MAKE IT

FOR THE TORTE

1. Preheat oven to 350°F. Oil a 10-inch cake pan and dust with almond flour.

2. In a medium bowl, whisk together eggs, maple syrup, and almond extract. Sift in almond flour and fold into egg mixture.

3. Pour batter into pan and sprinkle with slivered almonds. Bake for 40 minutes, until golden and firm to the touch.

FOR THE GELATO

1. In a small saucepan, warm milk and heavy cream slightly in a small saucepan. Set up double boiler using a separate pot.

2. In a medium bowl, whisk together maple sugar and yolks for 2–3 minutes, until light and fluffy.

3. Place over the double boiler and slowly stream in milk mixture, stirring vigorously until mixture thickens.

4. Cool, stir in almond extract, and churn in ice cream maker for approximately 20 minutes (this should be soft serve consistency). Transfer to freezer to firm up.

Dark Chocolate Beet Cakes

MAKES 6 SERVINGS

Rich and chocolaty, these gluten-free cakes are decadent enough for a special occasion. Puréed beets, which are barely detectable, add sweetness and a few extra grams of fiber and protein.

GATHER

- ½ cup (1 stick) unsalted butter, plus more for pan
- ½ cup almond flour, plus more for pan
- 2 beets (about 8 ounces), peeled and quartered
- 8 ounces (½ pound) bittersweet chocolate
- 2 teaspoons vanilla extract
- 4 large eggs, room temperature
- ¼ cup cane sugar
- ½ teaspoon kosher salt
- ¼ cup bittersweet chocolate chips

  Confectioners' sugar, for dusting

MAKE IT

1. Preheat the oven to 350°F. Butter and flour (using almond flour) a 12-cup muffin tin or mini Bundt cake pan.

2. Boil the beets until soft, 35–40 minutes, then drain and purée using a blender or food processor. Add 1 tablespoon cooking water to the beets, if necessary. Set aside to cool.

3. Melt the butter and chocolate in a bowl placed over a small pan of simmering water. (Do not let the water get into the chocolate.) Remove the melted mixture from the heat and add the vanilla extract. Set aside to cool.

4. Meanwhile, in the bowl of a stand mixer fitted with the paddle attachment, beat the eggs and sugar together for about 10 minutes, or until thick and pale. When you remove the paddle, thick ribbons should form from the batter coming off the paddle. Fold in the almond flour and salt.

5. Stir puréed beets into the chocolate mixture and fold that mixture into the egg mixture until it is fully incorporated. The mixture should be consistently dark and have no striations. Finally, stir in the chocolate chips. Evenly divide the batter between the cups of the prepared pan.

6. Bake for 20–25 minutes, or until a toothpick inserted into the center comes out clean. Remove pan from the oven and let cool for about 10 minutes. Then turn over the pan to release the cakes. Serve warm with a dusting of confectioners' sugar.

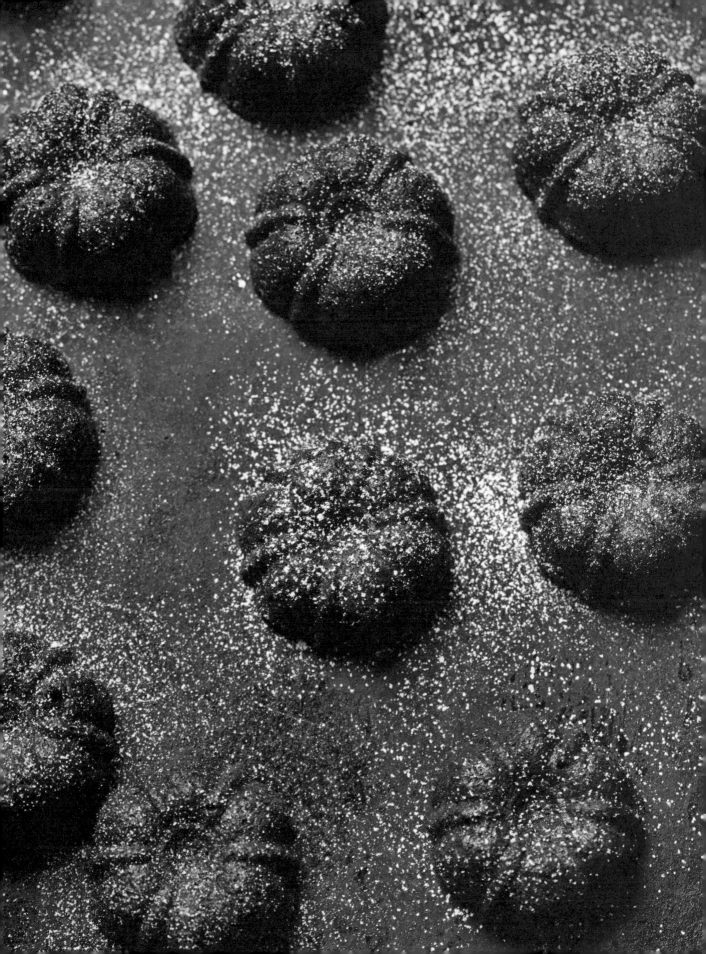

Sweet Pea Cupcakes with White Chocolate Frosting

MAKES 16 TO 18 CUPCAKES

Use frozen peas for a quick, convenient way to work in vegetables. The white chocolate frosting gains its cloud-like texture from the combination of agar and kudzu, natural plant-based thickeners. Agar is a natural gelling agent, derived from seaweed, and contains significant levels of fiber and minerals. Plus, the peas are small green powerhouses that rank high in vitamin C, vitamin E, vitamin K, and omega-3 content.

GATHER

SWEET PEA CUPCAKES

16 cupcake liners

3 organic eggs, room temperature

1½ cups organic cane sugar

1 teaspoon vanilla extract

2 cups frozen peas, thawed

⅓ cup boiling water

½ cup coconut oil, melted

2 tablespoons apple cider vinegar

2½ cups whole-wheat flour

Pinch of sea salt

1½ teaspoons baking powder

MAKE IT

FOR THE CUPCAKES

1. Preheat oven to 350°F. Line muffin pans with cupcake liners and set aside.

2. Add the eggs and sugar into a bowl and whisk with an electric hand mixer for 1–2 minutes until smooth and fluffy.

3. Add the vanilla extract, peas, water, oil, and vinegar to a high-speed blender, and purée until smooth. Fold into egg-sugar mixture until evenly combined.

4. In a separate bowl, sift the flour, salt, and baking powder. Whisk to combine.

5. Gently fold dry ingredients into wet, taking care not to overmix.

6. Pour batter into cupcake liners, until ¾ full. Bake for 15 minutes or until a toothpick comes out clean. Set on wire rack to cool.

WHITE CHOCOLATE FROSTING

4	teaspoons kudzu root
1/4	cup filtered water
1	(14-ounce) can coconut cream
2/3	cup agave syrup
	Pinch of sea salt
1	teaspoon vanilla extract
2	tablespoons agar flakes
1 1/2	cups white chocolate chips, plus extra for garnish
2	tablespoons coconut oil

FOR THE FROSTING

1. Add the kudzu and water to a small bowl and stir until smooth.

2. In a small pan, add the kudzu mixture, coconut cream, agave, salt, and vanilla extract and bring to a simmer. Fold in the agar flakes and continue to simmer for 5 minutes or until agar has dissolved.

3. Remove from heat and stir in the chocolate chips until completely melted.

4. Refrigerate until completely cool and firm.

5. Transfer cooled mixture into a food processor and pulse until fluffy.

6. Transfer mixture into a large piping bag and refrigerate until ready to frost cupcakes. Garnish with additional chocolate chips.

Golden Beet and Cinnamon Coffee Cake

MAKES APPROXIMATELY 9 SQUARES

What's not to love about kicking off your day with a coffee cake loaded with vitamin C, vitamin A, beta-carotene, and fiber? Golden beets elevate this classic favorite, packing in key nutrients and pairing effortlessly with the subtle cinnamon notes. A great way to utilize what you have on hand, feel free to substitute grated carrot, sweet potato, or butternut squash when making this coffee cake. The acid in the sour cream will help tenderize the gluten in the flour, helping keep your cake moist.

GATHER

FOR THE CRUMB TOPPING

¼ cup coconut oil, extra for greasing

⅓ cup whole-wheat pastry flour, extra for dusting dish

1 teaspoon ground cinnamon

¾ cup organic cane sugar

Pinch of sea salt

FOR THE CAKE

¾ cup coconut oil

¾ cup organic cane sugar

2 eggs

2 teaspoons vanilla extract

⅔ cup sour cream

¾ cup almond milk

MAKE IT

1. Preheat oven to 350°F. Grease 12 x 12-inch baking dish with coconut oil and dust with flour. Set aside.

2. In a medium bowl, form the crumb mixture by combining the coconut oil, flour, cinnamon, sugar, and salt and set aside.

3. To make the cake, add the coconut oil and sugar to a medium bowl and beat with electric hand mixer for 1 minute, or until fluffy. Incorporate the eggs, vanilla extract, sour cream, and almond milk, whisking until smooth.

4. In a separate bowl, sift the flour, salt, baking powder, and baking soda together. Add the grated golden beets, coating each piece with the flour mixture.

5. Fold the beet-flour mixture into wet ingredients, taking care not to overmix.

6. Pour half of batter into the greased dish and sprinkle on half the crumb mixture.

2	cups whole-wheat pastry flour
1/4	teaspoon salt
1	teaspoon baking powder
1	teaspoon baking soda
2	medium golden beets, peeled and grated (1 1/2 cups)

7. Pour in remaining mixture and top with remaining crumb mixture.

8. Bake for 40–45 minutes, or until toothpick comes out clean.

9. Cool coffee cake before slicing into squares.

Pineapple Strudel

MAKES 1 LOAF

This is one of those recipes that is so simple to make, but has an impressive end result. Avoid the temptation to buy precut fresh pineapple at the store; it costs more and it comes in wasteful single-use plastic. Instead, dive in and cut it yourself; there are plenty of tutorials online and you'll find when you do it the first time, you'll finish and wonder, "Why haven't I been doing this all along?" Have fun braiding the dough and make your pattern as pretty or as intricate as you want!

GATHER

1   whole pineapple, peeled, cored, and cut in to small cubes

1   cinnamon stick or $1/2$ teaspoon cinnamon

1   cup brown sugar

1   loaf commercial frozen whole-wheat bread dough thawed or 4 sheets frozen phyllo dough, thawed

MAKE IT

1. Heat a medium sauté pan and add pineapple, sugar, and cinnamon.

2. Cook pineapple on medium-high heat, stirring often until sugar melts and syrup is thick and golden in color, about 20 minutes. Pour into a medium glass bowl and let cool for 30 minutes.

3. Preheat oven to 375°F and lightly spray a large baking sheet.

4. On a clean surface, dust with flour to roll out dough.

5. Roll out dough $1/4$–$1/2$ inch thick. (If using phyllo dough, place 1 phyllo sheet on a flat dry surface. Lightly spray with vegetable oil, and lightly sprinkle with breadcrumbs. Repeat process until all 4 sheets are layered.)

6. Place cooled pineapple mixture in the center of the dough.

7. Fold and pinch dough together like a packet or braid dough. Carefully transfer to the baking sheet.

8. Set aside in a warm place to rise for 1 hour.

9. Bake for about 20–25 minutes.

Edible Petal Confetti Fun-fetti Birthday Cake

MAKES 1 CAKE

Obviously, this is not an everyday dessert you're going whip up.
But it is a pretty one that's perfect for any celebratory occasion. Be sure to use
pesticide-free flower petals for the garnish. Marigolds are hearty growers,
so when in doubt, you could just grow your own to be completely sure it's chemical-free.

GATHER

CONFETTI FUN-FETTI CAKE

1   cup coconut oil, melted, more to oil cake pans

3½ cups all-purpose flour, more to flour pans

2   teaspoons baking powder

2   teaspoons baking soda

¼   teaspoon sea salt

¾   cup freeze-dried raspberries, slightly crushed

1½ cups agave syrup

2   cups water

3   tablespoons vanilla extract

2   tablespoons apple cider vinegar

MAKE IT

FOR THE CAKE

1. Preheat oven to 325°F. Brush a thin layer of coconut oil onto 2 (9-inch) round cake pans, followed by a dusting of flour. Line each cake pan bottom with a circular piece of parchment paper.

2. In a large bowl, sift and whisk the flour, baking powder, baking soda, salt, and freeze-dried raspberries together.

3. In a separate bowl, combine the melted coconut oil, agave, water, vanilla extract, and vinegar.

4. Using a rubber spatula, fold the wet ingredients into the dry, just enough to combine. Do not overmix.

5. Pour mixture into cake pans and place on baking sheets. Bake for 35 minutes or until a toothpick comes out clean in the center of each cake. Cool cakes for 15 minutes before gently inverting them out of their pan onto a wire rack to completely cool.

6. Once cool, carefully slice each cake in half crosswise, using a serrated knife.

LEMON FROSTING

2   (14-ounce) cans coconut milk

    Pinch of sea salt

½   cup agar flakes

1   tablespoon lemon extract

1   cup agave syrup

1   cup cashews, soaked and drained

½   cup coconut oil, melted

TO ASSEMBLE

3   cups edible marigold petals, or edible flowers of choice

FOR THE FROSTING

1. Add coconut milk, salt, agar flakes, and lemon extract to a medium pot and bring to a simmer. Whisk to distribute agar and cook for 10–15 minutes, or until agar is completely dissolved.

2. In a high-speed blender, add the agave and soaked cashews and blend on high speed until completely smooth. Carefully stream in the melted coconut oil and warm coconut agar mixture.

3. Cool mixture completely until set in refrigerator, for approximately 1 hour. Pulse briefly in food processor, and transfer into piping bags or bowl.

TO ASSEMBLE

1. Add a thin layer of frosting between each layer of cake, along with a sprinkling of flower petals.

2. Once at 4 layers, spread a generous layer of frosting on the top and sides of the cake, using a spatula to smooth out whenever necessary.

3. Sprinkle frosting with flower petals.

Baked Miniature Donuts with Spirulina Sugar

MAKES 12 (2-INCH) DONUTS

I know, I know. I write about avoiding the need to buy special tools to make the recipes in this book, yet here I am telling you to invest in a donut pan. First, they aren't expensive. Second, they really help to keep the look and feel of a donut when making this recipe. If you want to make this without a donut pan, try transforming this from a donut recipe to a pancake one instead. By the way, we added spirulina—an algae found in lakes— to give this a nutritional boost; it adds color and protein and B vitamins.

GATHER

½ cup maple sugar, more to garnish

2 cups oat flour

1 tablespoon baking powder

1 tablespoon ground cinnamon

1 organic egg

1 (14-ounce) can coconut milk

TO GREASE PAN

1 teaspoon refined coconut oil

TO COAT

2 cup organic confectioners' sugar

2 tablespoons almond milk

¼ teaspoon spirulina, divided

MAKE IT

1. Preheat oven to 350°F.

2. Add the maple sugar, oat flour, baking powder, cinnamon, egg, and coconut milk to a blender and process until smooth.

3. Grease donut baking pans with coconut oil.

4. Pour batter in pan to fill each donut cavity ⅔ full (approximately ¼ cup per cavity) and bake for 10–12 minutes or until a toothpick comes out clean. Take out of oven and allow to cool.

5. In a small bowl, stir together the confectioners' sugar, almond milk, and a pinch of spirulina to make a glaze.

6. Dip each cooked donut in glaze and sprinkle with maple sugar and remaining spirulina.

Gluten-Free Coffee Tres Leche Cake

MAKES 1 (8-INCH) CAKE

When we photograph recipes for the pages of the magazine, we often do a lot
in a single day. And that means there's a lot of leftovers on the studio table for everyone
to share and take home at the end of the day . . . this cake is not one of them.
It was devoured in its entirely after the final frame was taken. It is that good.

GATHER

TRES LECHE CAKE

¾ cup melted unrefined coconut oil,
   more to oil pan

4 organic eggs

⅓ cup coconut nectar

⅔ cup coconut flour

2 tablespoons instant coffee

1 teaspoon baking powder

¼ teaspoon sea salt

¾ cup large coconut flakes

COCONUT-VANILLA FROSTING

½ cup coconut cream

¼ cup coconut sugar

1 cup coconut butter

1 vanilla bean, scraped

   Pinch of sea salt

MAKE IT

FOR THE CAKE

1. Preheat oven to 350°F. Brush an 8-inch cake pan interior
   with oil. Line bottom with parchment paper.

2. Add eggs, oil, and nectar to blender and process until smooth.

3. Add coconut flour, coffee, baking powder, and salt to blended
   mixture. Process until combined.

4. Transfer to pan, using a spatula to spread evenly.

5. Bake for 20 minutes or until lightly golden. Cool and remove
   from pan.

6. Spread coconut flakes on baking sheet and toast for
   5 minutes, or until golden.

7. Pour layer of Coffee Caramel onto cake and layer with
   Coconut-Vanilla Frosting. Drizzle with additional caramel
   and toasted coconut flakes.

FOR THE FROSTING

1. Use an electric hand or stand mixer to whip together the
   coconut cream, coconut sugar, coconut butter, scraped vanilla
   bean, and salt for 2–3 minutes, or until the mixture becomes
   stiff and fluffy.

2. Refrigerate frosting until ready to use.

COFFEE CARAMEL

1 (14-ounce) can coconut milk

3 tablespoons ground coffee

¼ cup coconut sugar

Pinch of sea salt

FOR THE CARAMEL

1. Add coconut milk and coffee to a pan and bring to a boil. Turn off heat and allow mixture to steep for 10 minutes.

2. Strain mixture through a fine-mesh strainer, discarding coffee. Rinse pan.

3. Return strained mixture to pan and stir in coconut sugar and salt.

4. Bring mixture to a simmer and cook for 5 minutes, or until mixture reduces and a caramel texture is formed. Cool completely before applying to cake.

Coffee Crepe-Layer Cake with Mocha Whipped Cream

MAKES 1 (10-LAYER) CREPE CAKE

This recipe works best with whole-wheat flour, but it can easily be made gluten-free by using a 1-for-1 alternative flour. And what's not to love? Layers of chocolate-y crepes with whipped cream kissed by mocha? It's as if a fancy restaurant was told "do something high-end that reminds you of Nutella." Here it is.

GATHER

COFFEE CREPE CAKE

1	(14-ounce) can coconut milk
¼	cup ground coffee
1	cup whole-wheat flour
3	organic eggs
	Pinch of sea salt
1	tablespoon refined coconut oil, for pan
1	cup hazelnuts, toasted and chopped

MAKE IT

FOR THE CAKE

1. Add coconut milk to a pan and stir in coffee. Bring to a boil.

2. Transfer mixture to a bowl and place in freezer for 15 minutes.

3. Strain mixture through a fine mesh strainer.

4. Add infused coconut milk, flour, eggs, and salt to a blender and process until smooth.

5. Refrigerate batter for 20 minutes. The consistency should be that of thin cream. Add water, as needed to thin out.

6. Heat nonstick pan over medium heat and spread with $1/2$ teaspoon coconut oil.

7. Pour in a few tablespoons of batter and swirl pan to spread into a thin layer. Cook for 2 minutes, or until edges start turning golden.

8. Use a spatula to flip crepe, and cook for an additional minute.

9. Remove crepe from pan and repeat process with remainder of batter.

MOCHA WHIPPED CREAM

2   tablespoons cocoa powder, more to garnish

3   tablespoons maple sugar, more to garnish

2   teaspoons instant coffee

     Pinch of sea salt

1   large can coconut cream (approximately 1 1/2 cups), chilled overnight

10. After crepes have completely cooled, spread 2 tablespoons of Mocha Whipped Cream on each layer along with a sprinkling of maple sugar, cocoa powder, and hazelnuts.

11. Stack layers to form a crepe cake. Top last layer with cocoa powder and maple sugar.

12. Use a sharp knife to cut into slices and serve.

FOR THE WHIPPED CREAM

1. Sift cocoa, maple sugar, coffee, and salt into a bowl.

2. Add coconut cream while using an electric hand mixer to whip into soft peaks.

3. Cover and refrigerate until ready to assemble crepe cake.

Matcha Gluten-Free Blondie Squares

MAKES 16 SQUARES

So, why matcha? Because it's a powerhouse tea that is brimming with antioxidants, helps your body detoxify, boosts metabolism, and tastes pretty darn good, too. If you have everything here but the matcha, by all means, make some killer blondie squares.

GATHER

3   cups almond flour

2   teaspoons baking powder

¼   teaspoon sea salt

½   cup coconut sugar, extra to dust

2   teaspoons matcha powder, extra to dust

½   cup coconut cream

⅓   cup almond butter

2   tablespoons vanilla extract

MAKE IT

1. Preheat oven to 350°F. Line an 8 x 8-inch baking pan with parchment paper.

2. Sift together almond flour, baking powder, salt, coconut sugar, and matcha powder into bowl.

3. Fold in coconut cream, almond butter, and vanilla extract.

4. Transfer to pan and bake for 20–25 minutes, or until golden and slightly firm to the touch.

5. Cool and cut into squares. Toss a pinch of matcha with a tablespoon of coconut sugar and sprinkle sugar mixture on top right before serving.

Orange-Quinoa Olive Oil Cake

MAKES 1 (10-INCH) CAKE

This is sticky, cakey, and bright and happy and perhaps one of the most beautiful cakes to make for a small gathering. Citrus is also a year-round crop, so this really can be made anytime. You can also infuse the syrups with fresh herbs to add a greater depth of flavor. And have fun! Experiment with other grains like millet or jasmine rice in lieu of quinoa.

GATHER

1   cup quinoa

$2\frac{3}{4}$ cups filtered water, divided

$1\frac{1}{3}$ cups olive oil

1   cup cassava flour

$1\frac{1}{2}$ teaspoons baking powder

$1\frac{1}{2}$ cups maple syrup

1   tablespoon vanilla extract

3   tablespoons ground flax seeds

    Pinch of sea salt

2   oranges

MAKE IT

1. Preheat oven to 350°F. Line bottom of a 10-inch cake pan with parchment paper. Brush sides with oil of choice.

2. Add quinoa and $1\frac{3}{4}$ cups filtered water to a small pan. Bring to a simmer, reduce heat to low, cover, and cook for 15 minutes. Cool slightly.

3. Add cooked quinoa, olive oil, cassava flour, baking powder, maple syrup, vanilla extract, ground flax seeds, salt, and remaining filtered water to a bowl and mix until combined.

4. Transfer mixture to cake pan and bake for 20 minutes or until top is firm and a toothpick comes out clean. Cool.

5. Remove peel and pith from oranges with a sharp knife. Cut into rounds.

6. Top cake with Citrus-Thyme Syrup and orange rounds.

CITRUS-THYME SYRUP

1	small bunch thyme
½	cup maple syrup
2	oranges

FOR SYRUP

1. Bruise thyme by hitting it with a wooden spoon until fragrant.

2. Add thyme and maple syrup to a small pan and bring to a simmer.

3. Allow to cook for 5 minutes. Zest and juice oranges, add to mixture, and cook for an additional 10 minutes on medium-low heat. Mixture should be gently bubbling.

4. Turn off heat and allow to steep for 20 minutes or until ready to use. Remove thyme sprigs.

Chocolate Quinoa Cake with Marshmallow Frosting

MAKES 1 (10-INCH) CAKE

One of the reasons we use pitted dates (in addition to adding sweetness) is it helps desserts take on more of a fudge-like consistency. This is a cake recipe that's also good on its own without frosting. And the frosting recipe is also one that's good to use on just about anything. Extra tip: Bake in an 8-inch pan if you want a cake with more height.

GATHER
CHOCOLATE QUINOA CAKE

1   cup quinoa flour

1   cup cacao powder

¾   cup coconut sugar

1½ teaspoons baking powder

     Pinch of sea salt

2   eggs

½   cup applesauce

8   pitted dates

¼   cup walnut oil

MAKE IT
FOR THE CAKE

1. Preheat oven to 350°F. Line bottom of a 10-inch cake pan with parchment paper. Brush sides with oil of choice.

2. Sift quinoa flour, cacao powder, coconut sugar, baking powder, and salt into a medium bowl. In a separate bowl, beat together eggs, applesauce, and walnut oil. Fold into flour mixture. Tear pitted dates into pieces and add to batter.

3. Transfer mixture into cake pan and bake for 30 minutes or until top is firm and a toothpick comes out clean. Cool.

4. Cut cake in half crosswise using a serrated knife. Once cake and frosting are completely cool, place half of the frosting on 1 layer of cake, top with second layer, and finish with remaining frosting.

MARSHMALLOW FROSTING

4   egg whites

½   teaspoon cream of tartar

1¾ cups agave nectar

2   teaspoons vanilla extract

FOR THE FROSTING

1. Whip together egg whites and cream of tartar in a stand mixer (or use an electric hand mixer) for 2 minutes or until stiff peaks form.

2. Bring agave nectar to a simmer in a small pan. Simmer for 2 minutes. Turn off heat and add vanilla extract.

3. Turn mixer on high, and slowly stream in hot agave into egg mixture allowing the egg mixture to pick up the hot sugar mixture before adding more. Mixture should double in size and become glossy.

4. Cool frosting in refrigerator for 30 minutes, or until chilled, before using for best results.

Paleo Sweet Potato Monkey Bread

MAKES 36 (1-TABLESPOON) PIECES

I've never been on a Paleo diet, but I sure know a lot of people who are and love to talk about it. A lot. And one thing I heard was how much they missed dessert and bread. So here's a recipe that's not only Paleo-friendly, but it satisfies that miss of sweet doughiness.

GATHER

- 2 medium sweet potatoes
- 1 tablespoon vanilla extract
- 1 (14-ounce) can full-fat coconut milk, divided
- 1¼ cups cassava flour
- ⅔ cup coconut flour
- 1 teaspoon baking powder
- ¼ teaspoon sea salt
- ½ cup coconut sugar
- 2 teaspoons ground cinnamon

MAKE IT

1. Preheat oven to 350°F.

2. Peel and cut sweet potatoes into small pieces. Place in pan, cover with water, bring to a boil, and cook for 10–15 minutes, or until tender. Drain and cool slightly.

3. Place cooked sweet potato (approximately 1¾ cups) into a blender along with vanilla extract, and 1 cup coconut milk. Process until well combined.

4. In a separate bowl, stir together the cassava flour, coconut flour, baking powder, and salt.

5. Slowly incorporate dry mixture into sweet potato mixture until a stiff dough forms. Roll dough into 1 tablespoon-size balls.

6. In a small bowl, stir together coconut sugar and cinnamon.

7. Roll each dough ball in sugar mixture and stack 4 balls into each cavity of a nonstick muffin tin (alternatively grease a pan that is not nonstick).

8. Bake for 15 minutes, or until bread is golden and cooked through.

9. Place remaining coconut milk, coconut sugar, and cinnamon mixture in a pan and bring to a simmer to create a cinnamon "fudge" for dipping.

Mini Paleo Cinnamon-Walnut Sticky Buns

MAKES 10 PIECES

Yes, psyllium husks are a laxative. But they are also a great binder to use in lieu of eggs when you're baking with it. It may seem weird to shop the local pharmacy for ingredients to bake with, but you'll be pleasantly surprised what a wonderful job it does to make these extraordinary walnut sticky buns.

GATHER

FOR THE DOUGH

3   tablespoons psyllium husks

1½ cups almond flour

1   teaspoon baking powder

Pinch of sea salt

½   cup coconut cream

1   tablespoon vanilla extract

FOR THE FILLING

½   cup walnuts

¼   cup pitted dates

1   tablespoon ground cinnamon

Pinch of sea salt

FOR THE GLAZE

¼   cup coconut cream

Pinch of ground cinnamon

MAKE IT

1. Preheat oven to 350°F. Line baking sheet with parchment paper.

2. In a medium bowl, add psyllium, almond flour, baking powder, and salt. Stir to combine. Incorporate coconut cream and vanilla extract until smooth dough forms. Allow to rest for 10 minutes.

3. Roll out dough into a ¼-inch-thick, roughly 6 x 12-inch rectangle on top of a piece of parchment paper.

4. To make the filling, chop walnuts and dates and mix with cinnamon and salt. Sprinkle mixture on top of dough.

5. Roll up and, using a sharp knife, cut roll into approximate 1-inch buns. If dough crumbles, use hands to gently press it back together into a bun form.

6. Lay onto baking sheet, leaving space between buns.

7. Bake for 15 minutes or until golden and cooked through. Carefully transfer to wire rack to cool for 10 minutes.

8. Mix coconut cream with cinnamon for the glaze.

9. Drizzle buns with glaze before serving and top with more cinnamon, if desired.

Pistachio-Cardamom Baklava Strudel

MAKES 8 PIECES

Any home cook will tell you that phyllo sheets are notoriously known for drying out quickly. So make sure to not skimp on the oil to prevent them from turning into dry, flaky sheets. You can also make this ahead of time: assembled strudel can be frozen before baking, and can go straight from the freezer to the oven.

GATHER

¾ cup shelled pistachios, plus extra for garnish

¼ teaspoon sea salt

1½ teaspoons ground cardamom

½ cup refined coconut oil

1 package whole-wheat phyllo dough

⅓ cup maple syrup

1 lemon, zested and juiced

MAKE IT

1. Preheat oven to 325°F.

2. Toast pistachios in oven for 5 minutes. Chop roughly, place in bowl, and sprinkle with salt and cardamom.

3. Briefly melt coconut oil in a small pan.

4. Place a piece of parchment paper on a baking sheet and brush with a layer of melted coconut oil.

5. Gently drape 3 pieces of phyllo dough onto the baking sheet and brush with additional oil.

6. Sprinkle half of the pistachio mixture on top of dough.

7. Repeat process by placing 3 more sheets, brushing with oil, and sprinkling on remaining pistachio mixture. Top with final 3 sheets of phyllo followed by oil.

8. Tightly roll layered phyllo into a long roll until a log is formed.

9. Score dough with a sharp knife into approximately 1 1/2-inch pieces.

10. Bake strudel for 25 minutes, or until golden and flaky. Cool slightly before cutting into pieces.

11. Simmer maple syrup in a pan for 5 minutes. Turn off heat and add the lemon zest and juice.

12. Drizzle syrup over strudel before serving and garnish with extra chopped pistachios.

A SWEET START

Calm down, Dr. Oz. I'm not talking about hot fudge sundaes first thing in the morning.

What this chapter is all about are sweet treats that make for the perfect start to your day and are also good for you and delicious, too.

Like I said in the introduction, I don't have the biggest sweet tooth. And even when I do, I prefer things that are slightly sweet and not over-the-top, sugar-busting decadent. So if you're someone like me, there are less sugary ideas to indulge in here when you want a little something, but not a whole lot of something.

And if you're cooking for a crowd for a holiday breakfast or a Sunday brunch, you can make big batches of almost anything here. These recipes are also very flexible, so if you want to swap out an ingredient for something you might have instead, by all means give it a whirl. Do the strawberries look mealy at the store? Go for the juicy peaches instead and make your breakfast poke bowl with a different fruit. No peanut butter? Use whatever nut butter you have for those energizing nut butter poppers. You get it: a sweet breakfast doesn't need to be stressful (nor should it). It should be a moment to set your day off in the right direction, and what better direction than something a little sweet, healthy, and happy?

Almost-Milkshake with Hemp and Hazelnut

MAKES 4 SERVINGS

You'll love this creamy drink's flavor combo of toasted hazelnut with a hint of agave sweetness. It's a perfect pick-me-up snack—and it's even better served over a bowl of crunchy granola.

GATHER

1   cup hemp seeds

2   cups hazelnuts, soaked and drained

6   cups water

1/3   cup agave nectar

1   teaspoon vanilla extract

Pinch of cinnamon

MAKE IT

1. Purée hemp seeds, hazelnuts, water, and agave in a high-powered blender until very smooth.

2. Add vanilla and cinnamon.

3. Process mixture in ice cream machine until partially frozen.

Note: If your kitchen is without an ice cream maker, treat this recipe as you would a granita: freeze the mixture and stir it every 15–20 minutes until it gets thick and milkshake-like.

Crunchy-Good Cardamom Granola

MAKES 8 SERVINGS

Not only is this granola easy to make, it is also
much more budget-friendly than buying it packaged. Serve it simply:
over plain yogurt, or with a very cold glass of almond milk.

GATHER

2	cups rolled oats
1	cup almonds
1	cup dried cherries, soaked in hot water for 10 minutes
½	cup maple syrup
¼	cup canola oil
1	teaspoon ground cardamom
1	teaspoon vanilla extract
1	teaspoon salt

MAKE IT

1. Preheat oven to 350°F. Line a baking sheet with parchment paper.

2. Combine oats, almonds, and cherries in a bowl.

3. Whisk together maple syrup, canola oil, cardamom, vanilla extract, and salt. Add wet ingredients to dry and mix thoroughly with spoon.

4. Transfer granola to baking sheet and bake until crisp and golden, stirring frequently, approximately 20–25 minutes.

Breakfast Cookies

MAKES 20 COOKIES

My good friend Catherine McCord has a prolific website and social media following under the name Weelicious. Her mission has been to make cooking healthy food for kids a breeze, all while giving great flavor that can even please a grown-up palate. My all-time favorite recipe she's shared with us are these breakfast cookies. Yes, they are shaped like a cookie and taste like one, but they're loaded with nutrition to get your morning off on the right start.

GATHER

¼ cup unsalted butter, softened

½ cup applesauce

½ cup maple syrup

1 large egg

2 teaspoons vanilla extract

1 cup whole-wheat flour

2 cups old-fashioned oats

½ teaspoon baking soda

½ teaspoon salt

1 teaspoon ground cinnamon

½ cup shelled pistachios

½ cup dried cherries

½ cup flax seeds

MAKE IT

1. Preheat oven to 350°F. Line 2 baking sheets with Silpat or parchment paper.

2. Place the butter, applesauce, and maple syrup in a bowl or standing mixer and beat until well combined.

3. Add the egg and vanilla extract and beat until smooth.

4. In a separate bowl, whisk together the flour, oats, baking soda, salt, and cinnamon.

5. Slowly add dry ingredients into wet and mix to incorporate.

6. Fold in the pistachios, cherries, and flax seeds.

7. Using a small ice cream scoop or 2-tablespoon measure, drop dough onto baking sheets. Use the palm of your hand to gently press down the cookies, as they do not spread during baking.

8. Bake for 15 minutes and remove to a wire rack to cool.

Banana-Pecan Overnight Oats

MAKES 2 SERVINGS

What could be easier than dumping everything into a jar and
letting it "cook" itself overnight? The juxtaposition of creamy, cold oats with
warm ooey, gooey bananas makes for a tasty treat to start the day.

GATHER

½   cup rolled oats

½   cup almond milk

1   cup vanilla yogurt

1   tablespoon honey, or sweetener
of choice

1   tablespoon coconut oil

1   banana, sliced into ¼-inch rounds

½   teaspoon cinnamon

Pinch of sea salt

¼   cup pecans

MAKE IT

1. Combine rolled oats, almond milk, yogurt, and honey in a medium bowl or jar. Cover and refrigerate overnight.

2. In nonstick pan, warm coconut oil over medium heat. Add banana slices in a single layer and cook for 1 minute per side or until golden.

3. Retrieve oat mixture, and stir in cinnamon and salt.

4. Garnish with bananas and pecans.

Yogurt Bowl with Brûléed Bananas and Mint

MAKES 1 BOWL

My good friend, nutritionist Adam Rosante, is a fan of the surprise ingredient here: coconut oil. He says, "It has the ability to boost thyroid function which can help increase your metabolism and endurance. If you're looking to lean out and power your workouts, this can really help."

GATHER

½ teaspoon raw coconut oil

1 banana, peeled and cut into ½-inch slices

½ teaspoon maple crystals or another granulated sweetener

1 cup plain yogurt

A few mint leaves

MAKE IT

1. Add coconut oil to a medium skillet over medium-low heat. Add bananas and sweetener, toss to combine, and cook until bananas begin to soften and brown in places, about 5–7 minutes.

2. Place yogurt in a serving bowl; top with bananas and mint.

Sweet Potato-Peach Smoothie

MAKES 1 TO 2 SERVINGS

One of my go-to authorities on healthy living is author and expert Candice Kumai. This is my favorite recipe of hers because it's really delicious and super nutritious! Candice says this smoothie is "packed with beta-carotene, the anti-oxidants in this smoothie make it a real standout that can also help to keep your blood sugar in check."

GATHER

2½ cups almond milk

½ frozen banana

¾ cup cooked sweet potato

3 cups frozen peaches

¼ teaspoon pumpkin spice

¼ teaspoon nutmeg

¼ teaspoon cinnamon

MAKE IT

Mix all of the ingredients in a blender until smooth consistency. Enjoy immediately.

Peanut Butter Poppers

MAKES 12 POPPERS

If you regularly skip breakfast, consider ways to work it into your routine—like now.
Studies have shown that eating breakfast boosts brain power and energy levels,
and helps prevent overeating the rest of the day, too. This recipe can be made in big
batches, and it stores well in the fridge. Just grab a few and go in the morning!

GATHER

1   cup oats

⅔   cup unsweetened coconut

½   cup peanut butter

½   cup ground flax seeds

½   cup semisweet chocolate chips

⅓   cup honey

1   teaspoon vanilla extract

1   tablespoon chia seeds

MAKE IT

1. Combine all ingredients and refrigerate until firm. Form into 12 equal-size balls.

2. Leftovers? Just store them in an airtight container in the refrigerator.

Pumpkin Waffles

MAKES 6 SERVINGS

What do you do when you have leftover pumpkin purée?
You make these super tasty waffles, that's what!

GATHER

½ cup unsweetened pumpkin purée

3 eggs, separated

1 cup whole milk

4 tablespoons butter, melted

1 cup whole-wheat pastry flour

2 tablespoons fine cornmeal

2 teaspoons baking powder

2 tablespoons maple crystals, or organic granulated sugar

½ teaspoon sea salt

Plain yogurt, to serve

Fresh fruit, to serve

MAKE IT

1. Preheat a waffle iron according to manufacturer's directions.

2. In a large bowl, whisk together pumpkin, egg yolks, milk, and butter.

3. In a separate bowl, combine flour, cornmeal, baking powder, maple crystals, and salt.

4. Pour the wet ingredients into the dry, and mix with a rubber spatula, just until combined.

5. Whisk the egg whites with a hand mixer or whisk to soft peaks. Fold whipped whites into the mixed batter. Cook waffles according to manufacturer's directions.

6. Serve warm, with yogurt and fruit.

Note: Freeze cool waffles to enjoy throughout the week. To reheat, place frozen waffle into toaster oven for 5–7 minutes.

Carrot Cake Pancake Stack with Raisin Butter

MAKES 15 SMALL PANCAKES

Carrot cake is one of my all-time favorite desserts, so this nod, in pancake form, is one of my favorite breakfast treats to indulge in. If you want to amp these up and bring in that cream cheese frosting, just slather some cream cheese in between stacks with dobs of the delicious raisin butter swirled in. Yum!

GATHER

RAISIN BUTTER

2 tablespoons golden raisins

2 tablespoons raisins

¼ cup unsalted butter, softened

Pinch of sea salt

CARROT CAKE PANCAKES

1¼ cups whole-wheat flour

½ cup walnuts, chopped plus extra for garnish

2 teaspoons baking powder

2 teaspoons ground allspice

Pinch of sea salt

2 large carrots, peeled and finely grated (approximately 1 cup)

¼ cup maple syrup

1 cup coconut water

2 teaspoons vanilla extract

2 eggs

1 tablespoon refined coconut oil, for brushing pan

MAKE IT

FOR THE BUTTER

1. In a small bowl, stir together the 2 varieties of raisins, butter and salt.

2. If desired, form into a log or scoop into medallions.

3. Refrigerate raisin butter until ready to serve.

FOR THE PANCAKES

1 In a medium bowl, whisk together the flour, walnuts, baking powder, allspice, and salt.

2. Add the carrot to the flour mixture, using hands to evenly distribute and ensure there are no remaining large lumps of grated carrot.

3. In a separate bowl, whisk together the maple syrup, coconut water, vanilla extract, and eggs. Gradually pour into the dry mixture, using a rubber spatula to gently form a batter. Do not overmix.

4. Preheat a large nonstick pan or griddle over medium heat and brush lightly with oil.

5. Place 2 spoonfuls of batter to form a round, 3-inch pancake. Repeat process to fill pan, taking care not overcrowd.

6. Flip pancakes after approximately 2 minutes, and cook for 1 minute longer.

7. Remove from pan and repeat process with remainder of batter, working in batches.

8. Serve pancakes hot with raisin butter and garnished with walnut pieces.

Golden Turmeric Oats with Crushed Pistachios and Rose Water

MAKES 3 CUPS

I personally love the unexpected floral notes rose water adds to this recipe, but for many it can conjure up memories of Grandma's perfume. It's perfectly fine to omit entirely if you want to!

GATHER

1½ cups rolled oats

1 cup coconut milk

2½ cups filtered water

½ teaspoon turmeric powder

½ teaspoon ground cardamom

Pinch of sea salt

3 teaspoons rose water

¼ cup maple syrup, or to taste

¼ cup pistachios, finely chopped

MAKE IT

1. Add rolled oats, coconut milk, water, turmeric, cardamom, and salt to a saucepan and bring mixture to a boil over medium heat.

2. Reduce mixture to a simmer and cook for 15–20 minutes, or until tender, stirring occasionally.

3. Stir in rose water and maple syrup. Transfer into bowl and top with pistachios.

Breakfast Poke Bowl

MAKES 2 SERVINGS

Don't skip the step with the fresh ginger and strawberries. It may not look like an important part of the recipe, but it's vital. Something magical happens when the acidity of ginger hits the fresh strawberries; it brightens the flavor and makes them extra juicy in this poke bowl. This is also an easy recipe to double, triple—heck—quadruple if you want to.

GATHER

1 cup jasmine rice

3 cups unsweetened almond milk, divided

Pinch of sea salt

1 tablespoon matcha powder

3 tablespoons maple syrup

2 cups strawberries, stemmed and cut into rounds

1 (2-inch) piece ginger root

2 teaspoons black sesame seeds

MAKE IT

1. Add rice, $2^{1}/_{2}$ cups almond milk and salt to a small pot. Stir to combine and bring mixture to a simmer over medium heat.

2. Reduce heat, cover pot, and cook rice for 15 minutes, stirring occasionally.

3. Blend or thoroughly whisk together the remaining almond milk with the matcha and maple syrup, and fold into cooked rice. Rice can be served hot, at room temperature, or chilled.

4. Peel and grate ginger on the large setting of a box grater and squeeze between hands or through cheesecloth to extract juice (approximately 1 tablespoon). Discard ginger pulp.

5. Gently toss strawberries with ginger juice. Allow mixture to marinate for a few minutes.

6. Toast sesame seeds by placing in a small pan and warming over low heat for 1 minute, or until seeds become fragrant.

7. Place rice into bowls and top with ginger-macerated strawberries and toasted black sesame seeds.

Flavored Almond Milk

MAKES 2$\frac{1}{2}$ CUPS

If you really wanted to, you could have small bowls with all of these powders so people can mix their own custom flavor of homemade almond milk at a breakfast bar. Or, you can just pick one and make a giant pitcher of the freshest, cleanest, and most delicious flavored almond milk. Try the milk over cereal, hot oatmeal, or even a splash in your coffee.

GATHER

FOR THE ALMOND MILK BASE

$\frac{1}{2}$ cup blanched almonds, soaked

3   cups filtered water

3   Medjool dates, pitted

     Pinch of sea salt

OPTIONAL ADD-INS (CHOOSE ONE)

$\frac{3}{4}$ cup freeze-dried raspberries

1   teaspoon turmeric powder

$\frac{1}{2}$ teaspoon blue algae powder

2   teaspoons matcha powder

1   tablespoon acai powder, with
     1 tablespoon lemon juice

MAKE IT

1. Drain and rinse almonds and place in a high-speed blender along with water, pitted dates, and salt.

2. Process mixture for 30 seconds and strain through cheesecloth or a fine mesh bag to remove pulp. Discard pulp or reserve for another use.

3. Rinse blender and process strained milk with 1 add-in for 20 seconds or until smooth. Serve flavored milk warm or chilled.

Cherry, Avocado, and Pistachio Granola Bars

MAKES 9 BARS

These granola bars don't have to be in bar shape; you can use an ice cream scoop to make them into small balls that can be like little raw truffles. Also, the nori—which is a dried seaweed and loaded with good-for-you minerals— can be bitter, so you can omit if it's something a younger palate may not enjoy.

GATHER

1½ cups pistachios

1 sheet dried nori

¾ cup dried tart cherries

1 cup Medjool dates, pits removed

1 ripe avocado

½ teaspoon sea salt

½ cup filtered water

¾ cup hemp seeds

MAKE IT

1. Preheat oven to 325°F.

2. Spread pistachios and nori on a baking sheet and toast for 5 minutes.

3. Add pistachios and nori to a food processor and pulse until coarsely ground.

4. Transfer mixture to bowl and toss with cherries.

5. Add pitted dates, avocado, salt, and water to food processor and pulse until a paste forms.

6. Mix together the avocado-date paste with the pistachio-cherry mixture.

7. Using hands, mold the mixture into 1 x 3-inch bars. Roll each in hemp seeds and place on a rack-lined baking tray.

8. Bake for 25–30 minutes, or until the hemp seeds are lightly golden. Alternatively, dehydrate bars in a dehydrator for a few hours.

9. Allow bars to cool for a few minutes, before lifting. Cool completely and keep in an airtight container for 5–7 days.

Coffee Smoothie

SERVES 1

I love this smoothie because sometimes all you realistically have
time for is a coffee, and it can be difficult to have coffee on an empty stomach.
The coconut milk and chia seeds will actually help fill you up.
If you aren't a fan of caffeine, you can easily swap it out for decaf.

GATHER

½ cup iced coffee

½ cup hemp milk

½ unripe banana, frozen (optional)

2 teaspoons chia seeds

1 teaspoon coconut oil

1 teaspoon cocoa powder

½ teaspoon vanilla extract

Handful of ice cubes

MAKE IT

Combine ingredients in blender and blend until smooth.

Raspberry, Chocolate, and Almond Cereal Bars

MAKES 12 BARS

Here's a great "to go" bar that replaces those store-bought cereal bars with one that's healthier and tastes a whole lot better. It can be hard to find freeze-dried raspberries, so you can look in the bulk section of your supermarket to replace it with dried fruit.

GATHER

- 1 (1.3-ounce) package freeze-dried raspberries
- 3/4 cup dark chocolate chips
- 1 cup sliced almonds, extra for garnish
- 3 cups puffed cereal
- 1 1/2 cups brown rice syrup
- 1 tablespoon vanilla extract

  Pinch of flaky sea salt, extra for garnish

MAKE IT

1. Gently crumble raspberries (approximately 1 1/2 cups) into medium bowl, reserving a handful for garnish. Add chocolate chips, sliced almonds, and puffed cereal.

2. Add rice syrup, vanilla extract, and salt to a small pan and warm on low heat for 1 minute or until mixture bubbles and becomes molten.

3. Slowly pour over raspberry mixture, stirring until evenly distributed and chocolate chips melt.

4. Press into an 8 x 8-inch pan lined with parchment paper and garnish with almonds, raspberries, and a sprinkling of salt.

5. Cool in refrigerator for 20 minutes and cut into bars.

THE CHOCOLATE FACTORY

Loaded with a powerful source of antioxidants, chocolate should have a recurring role in your weekly grocery list. It's been known to lower blood pressure and help reduce the risk of heart disease. And let's face it—it's delicious. Addictively, passionately, Charlie-and-the-Chocolate-Factory delicious.

But like everything in life, chocolate needs to be eaten in moderation, because the best treats load in sugar and fats that can derail nutrition goals. We have the gamut of chocolate-loving recipes in this chapter, from a simple bark to a keto-friendly chocolate avocado bread that can be dressed up to be sweet or savory. With these chocolate-friendly recipes, I hope you'll expand your horizons on what cocoa can do in surprising ways, one chip at a time.

The Everything Chocolate Bark

MAKES 12 SERVINGS

Rich chocolate meets pumpkin seeds, dried apricots, and
sea salt to offer up a bulk-bin-based treat that's simultaneously sweet,
bitter, salty, and tangy—super complex, but perfectly balanced.

GATHER

- ¾ pound semisweet chocolate (chips or chopped), divided
- ½ cup pumpkin seeds
- ½ cup dried apricots, chopped
- 2 tablespoons coarse sea salt

MAKE IT

1. Place ½ pound chocolate in metal bowl set over simmering water.

2. Melt chocolate, stirring constantly, until very smooth (115°F, as read via candy thermometer). Remove bowl from heat.

3. Whisk remaining chocolate into melted chocolate until completely dissolved and smooth. Continue whisking until chocolate is just warm (88°F).

4. Pour melted chocolate onto parchment-lined baking sheet. Spread evenly with spatula. Sprinkle surface with pumpkin seeds, chopped apricots, and sea salt. Cool bark until set.

Party-Perfect Chocolate and Coconut Truffles

MAKES 32 TRUFFLES

Always a crowd-pleaser, these sweet-but-not-too-sweet treats should be savored—
but we guarantee they'll be gone in a flash. Serve them with after-dinner drinks
or use them as easy (and inexpensive) thank-you gifts for guests.

GATHER

1   cup coconut

1½ cups raw walnuts, soaked
     overnight and drained

¼   teaspoon sea salt

½   pound pitted dates

½   cup unsweetened cocoa powder

1   teaspoon vanilla extract

MAKE IT

1. Preheat oven to 350°F. Toast coconut until lightly golden,
   approximately 5 minutes. Set aside to cool.

2. Combine walnuts and salt in food processor. Process until
   finely ground. Add dates, cocoa powder, and vanilla extract.
   Process until mixture binds.

3. Using a 1-ounce ice cream scoop, scoop individual truffles
   and roll them in toasted coconut.

Cacao-Mulberry Squares

MAKES APPROXIMATELY 16 SQUARES

I love these squares because even though there are just a handful of ingredients, they pack a powerful tasty punch. If you haven't had mulberries, you should—they are a good source of iron and vitamin C and have been linked to help lower cholesterol and blood sugar.

GATHER

3 cups raw walnuts, soaked overnight and drained (3 3/4 cups)

1/8 teaspoon sea salt

1 pound Medjool dates, pitted and chopped

1 cup dried mulberries, pitted and soaked 10 minutes in warm water

2/3 cup unsweetened cacao powder

2 teaspoons almond extract

MAKE IT

1. Place half of the walnuts and salt in food processor and process until finely ground. Add half the dates, mulberries, cocoa powder, and almond extract and process until mixture begins to stick together. Transfer to large mixing bowl. Repeat with remaining ingredients and combine them together.

2. Using a rolling pin, roll mixture evenly to 1/2-inch thickness between 2 sheets of parchment paper. You can transfer the parchment-lined mixture to a baking sheet for ease of chilling if desired.

3. Chill mixture 15 minutes or until firm then cut with a sharp knife into desired sizes or cut with round or other shaped cookie cutters. Chill until ready to plate and serve.

White Chocolate and Matcha Microwave Popcorn

MAKES 1 BIG BOWL

Not all popcorn has to be buttery and salty. Here's an alternative that uses the antioxidant powerhouse matcha paired with melted white chocolate for a marriage that's made in movie heaven.

GATHER

⅓ cup popcorn kernels

2 tablespoons coconut oil, divided

1 brown paper bag

1 cup white chocolate chips

½ teaspoon coarse sea salt

2 tablespoons matcha powder

MAKE IT

1. In medium bowl, lightly coat kernels with small amount of coconut oil (about ½ teaspoon).

2. Place in paper bag, folding the end of the bag a few times to create a durable seal (important so bag does not open during popping).

3. Place bag in microwave and cook for 2 minutes, or until 2–3 seconds pass between popping sounds. Remove carefully, bag will be hot.

4. Place white chocolate chips and remaining coconut oil in small microwave-safe bowl.

5. Microwave chocolate for 20–30 seconds, or just until melted.

6. Toss popcorn with melted white chocolate and sea salt. Gently sprinkle with matcha powder.

Dark Chocolate Truffles with Black Lava Rock Salt

MAKES 4 TO 6 SERVINGS

Dark chocolate has been proven to be a good source of antioxidants, so a bite or two a day can help improve your health. But even with its health benefits, these should be consumed in moderation.

GATHER

TRUFFLE BATTER

½ cup full-fat coconut milk

1   tablespoon coconut oil

½ teaspoon vanilla extract

    Pinch of sea salt

8   ounces bittersweet chocolate chips

TRUFFLE TOPPING

1   cup water

12 ounces bittersweet chocolate chips, divided

2   tablespoons black lava rock salt

MAKE IT

FOR THE BATTER

1. Add the coconut milk, coconut oil, vanilla extract, and salt to a small saucepan and bring to a simmer.

2. Add the chocolate chips to a medium bowl and pour in hot coconut mixture. Stir until the chocolate has completely melted.

3. Refrigerate mixture for 30 minutes, or until firm to the touch.

4. Use a tablespoon measuring spoon to scoop and portion batter. Gently roll each piece of batter between hands to form sphere.

FOR THE TOPPING

1. Bring a small saucepan with water to a simmer. Place a heat-proof bowl over the pan and melt half of the chocolate chips.

2. Remove bowl with melted chocolate off heat and add in remaining chocolate, to temper the melted chocolate. Stir until all the chocolate is melted.

3. Dip each piece of rolled truffle batter into the chocolate using a metal spoon to help drape the batter with a layer of chocolate. Place coated truffle on a parchment-lined tray, and sprinkle the top of the truffle with a small amount of black lava rock salt.

4. Repeat with remaining batter and keep refrigerated until ready to serve.

Eggplant Fudge Bars

MAKES APPROXIMATELY 12 SQUARES

These bars take the prize for their decadent nature and also rank high in antioxidant content. The luxurious silkiness comes from blending a half-pound of cooked eggplant with coconut oil and bittersweet dark chocolate. Make sure to peel the eggplant and purée it long enough to break up any seeds. And not only is almond flour gluten-free, it's also high in fiber, protein, vitamin E, and magnesium.

GATHER

6	tablespoons coconut oil, more to grease baking dish
1	medium eggplant (approximately ½ pound), peeled and diced
2	cups filtered water
1	cup bittersweet chocolate pieces (approximately 6 ounces)
1	teaspoon vanilla extract
½	cup coconut sugar
½	cup almond flour
⅓	cup cacao powder
½	teaspoon baking powder
¼	teaspoon sea salt
2	organic eggs, beaten
¼	cup pitted dates, torn into pieces

MAKE IT

1. Preheat oven to 350°F. Grease a 12 x 12-inch baking dish with coconut oil. Cover bottom of dish with piece of parchment paper.

2. Place the diced eggplant and water into a small pan and bring to a boil. Lower heat and simmer for 5 minutes, or until tender. Drain thoroughly.

3. Add the warm eggplant to a high-speed blender, along with coconut oil, chocolate pieces, and vanilla extract, and blend until smooth.

4. In a medium bowl, whisk together the coconut sugar, almond flour, cacao powder, baking powder, and salt. Add to blender and purée until smooth.

5. Transfer mixture into bowl and fold in eggs and date pieces.

6. Pour batter into greased baking dish and bake for 40–45 minutes or until a toothpick comes out clean.

7. Chill completely in refrigerator before cutting into squares.

Black Forest-Avocado Mousse with Macerated Cherries and Cacao Nibs

MAKES 2 SERVINGS

I love the combination of ingredients in this chocolate mousse recipe: the bitterness of the coffee and brandy pair exceptionally well with the richness of the avocado and maple syrup. If you'd like to give this mousse an extra kick, you can replace the coffee with espresso instead.

GATHER

FOR THE MOUSSE

2 ripe avocados, pitted and peeled

1/3 cup strong-brewed coffee

1/4 cup maple syrup

1 teaspoon vanilla extract

Pinch of sea salt

1/4 cup cocoa powder

FOR THE MACERATED CHERRIES

3/4 cup dried tart cherries

3 tablespoons brandy

1/2 cup filtered water

FOR THE GARNISH

2 tablespoons cacao nibs

MAKE IT

1. Add avocados, coffee, maple syrup, vanilla extract, and salt to a food processor, processing until smooth. Mix in cocoa powder and pulse until combined.

2. Chill avocado mousse and serving ware for 30 minutes.

3. Place cherries, brandy, and water into a small saucepan and bring to simmer for 2 minutes or until cherries have absorbed all the liquid.

4. Fold 1/3 cup macerated cherries into the avocado mousse, reserving rest for garnish.

5. Scoop into bowls and top with remaining macerated cherries and cacao nibs.

Dark Chocolate Matcha Nut Butter Cups

MAKES 8 PIECES

It's not a typo, there is miso paste in this recipe. Miso adds a bit of saltiness and umami richness that elevates a simple combo of chocolate and nut butter into something more elevated and unexpected. If you don't have tahini, you can use different nut and seed butters like sunflower, cashew, or almond.

GATHER

FOR THE FILLING

2 tablespoons cashews

$\frac{1}{3}$ cup tahini

$1\frac{1}{2}$ teaspoons miso paste

1 teaspoon matcha powder, more for garnish

$1\frac{1}{2}$ tablespoons maple syrup

FOR THE CHOCOLATE COATING

$\frac{3}{4}$ cup refined coconut oil

$\frac{3}{4}$ cup cocoa powder

$\frac{1}{4}$ cup maple syrup

FOR THE GARNISH

1 teaspoon flaky sea salt

MAKE IT

1. Finely chop cashews and place in a bowl with tahini, miso, matcha, and maple syrup. Stir to combine and refrigerate for 10 minutes or until mixture firms up.

2. Melt coconut oil and stir in cocoa powder and maple syrup to make coating.

3. Place 8 cupcake liners into a muffin tin.

4. Place 1 tablespoon of chocolate coating into each cupcake liner, and freeze for 5 minutes.

5. Flatten filling into 8 discs just smaller than the bottom of the cupcake liners and place onto set chocolate, leaving a border. Pour an additional tablespoon of chocolate coating on each filling disc.

6. Toss salt with a pinch of matcha powder and use to garnish butter cups.

7. Freeze for an additional 10 minutes or until chocolate solidifies.

8. Keep nut butter cups either refrigerated or frozen.

Winter Matcha Peppermint Patties

MAKES 8 PIECES

Make sure you buy unsweetened and finely shredded coconut for this recipe so the mouth feel is more candy-like and not chunky. And keep in mind the peppermint extract is very strong, so if you'd like something less minty, use less and adjust to taste.

GATHER

1¼ cups finely shredded unsweetened coconut

½ cup coconut butter

¼ cup maple syrup

¼ teaspoon peppermint extract

½ teaspoon matcha powder

1 cup dark chocolate chips

MAKE IT

1. In a medium bowl, add shredded coconut, coconut butter, maple syrup, and peppermint extract. Stir until thoroughly combined. Evenly divide batter into 2 bowls and fold matcha into 1 bowl of batter.

2. Form batter into 2-tablespoon-size discs by taking 1 tablespoon of each batter and pressing together, using hands to manipulate batter. Place in freezer for 10 minutes, or until completely frozen.

3. Melt ½ cup of chocolate chips over double boiler. Remove from heat and stir in remaining chocolate to temper mixture.

4. Spoon chocolate over each disc until the top and sides are covered and place on a parchment paper-lined plate. Freeze for additional 5 minutes.

Almond Flour "Twix"

MAKES 16 FUN-SIZE BARS

We all crave flavors that are the most familiar to us as well as the most flavorful. Unfortunately, that fact can lead to some unhealthy choices like candy bars found at the convenience store. This is an alternative to the ubiquitous Twix candy bar that's gluten-free and totally plant-based, too.

GATHER

¼ cup refined coconut oil

3 cups almond flour

¼ cup arrowroot

¼ cup maple syrup

1 cup Medjool dates

3 tablespoons salted almond butter

2 cups dark chocolate chips

MAKE IT

1. Preheat oven to 325°F.

2. Mix together coconut oil, almond flour, arrowroot, and maple syrup in a bowl, evenly distributing the oil and syrup.

3. Line an 8 x 8-inch baking dish with parchment paper and firmly press in crust mixture. Bake for 20 minutes or until lightly golden.

4. Pit dates and soak in hot water for 10 minutes. Blend dates with almond butter and 1/2 cup soaking water until a smooth paste forms.

5. Pour date paste over baked layer and bake for additional 20 minutes.

6. Cool slightly and remove from pan.

7. Slice into 1 x 2-inch bars, wiping down knife between cuts.

8. Melt half of chocolate chips in pan over medium heat just until melted. Turn off heat and stir in remaining chocolate until melted.

9. Drizzle chocolate over bars and refrigerate until bars are set.

Keto White Chocolate-Macadamia Fudge

MAKES APPROXIMATELY 24 PIECES

Good fat is not an oxymoron. Neither is a vegan keto diet. If you're on keto, this fudge can satisfy your sweet tooth and also help you stay in ketosis to burn fat and keep you energized. It's less boardwalk fudge and more fat bomb, but it is super delicious.

GATHER

1   cup unsalted macadamia nuts

¾   cup freeze-dried blueberries

1   cup cacao butter

1   cup coconut butter

2   tablespoons vanilla extract

½   teaspoon sea salt

MAKE IT

1. Chop macadamia nuts and freeze-dried blueberries.

2. Warm cacao butter in a small pan for 30 seconds or until just melted and remove from heat.

3. Add coconut butter, vanilla extract, and salt to a food processor and process until smooth, streaming in cacao butter as machine is running.

4. Pour mixture into small round silicone molds and top with a layer of chopped macadamia nuts and crumbled blueberries. Or if you don't have molds, pour mixture into a lightly greased pan and top with nuts and berries.

5. Set in freezer for 30 minutes or until firm. Remove from molds or slice into pieces.

Dark Chocolate Avocado Bread

MAKES 1 MEDIUM LOAF

Believe it or not, this is a chocolate bread that is totally keto-friendly.
The combination of good fats from the avocados, protein from the eggs, and the low-carb
flour from almonds magically all comes together to make a dense, chocolatey bread.
Note: bread can be left unsweetened and served with savory items, too.

GATHER

3 tablespoons avocado oil,
more for pan

2 ripe avocados

3 organic eggs

6 pitted dates

2¼ cups almond flour

¼ cup cocoa powder, extra for
dusting

1½ teaspoons baking powder

¾ cup maple syrup

MAKE IT

1. Preheat oven to 350°F. Line a loaf pan with parchment paper.
Brush lightly with avocado oil.

2. Add avocado oil, avocados, eggs, and dates to blender. Process
until smooth.

3. Add almond flour, cocoa powder, and baking powder to a bowl.

4. Stir in puréed avocado mixture until evenly combined.

5. Pour mixture into loaf pan and bake for 30–40 minutes, or
until cooked through. Use a toothpick to test for doneness; if
it comes out clean, it's cooked through.

SWEET UN-NOTHINGS

For as sweet as they are, desserts are more than just sugary concoctions to end a meal. And sometimes you have all-star treats that aren't quite a cookie, a frozen treat, or a chocolate lover's dream come true. But underneath their sugary surface, they are still great to eat.

This chapter is a mix of amazing recipes that cover the gamut, and most can be described in a single word: fudge, fluff, bark, jerky, and more. And we're talking sticky toasted fudge that's reminiscent of what you'd find on the boardwalk in New Jersey. Or a three-ingredient marshmallow fluff that's fantastic on ice cream sundaes or summer cobbler. And even a sticky, sweet, and savory jerky made from—wait for it—dehydrated watermelon. Yes, watermelon jerky. *And it's divine.*

Maca and Toasted Almond Fudge

MAKES 1 (8 X 8-INCH) SQUARE OR ABOUT 16 SERVINGS

Maca has long been known as "Peruvian ginseng" because of its natural energizing properties. It's a radish root with very little taste that works well in this sweet recipe. You'll find it in powder form at most health food stores.

GATHER

1¾ cups blanched almonds

¼ cup maca powder

2 cups almond milk

¾ cup maple crystals

Pinch of salt

2 tablespoons coconut oil, melted

MAKE IT

1. Grind the almonds in a food processor until they become a fine powder. Transfer to a medium bowl and whisk in the maca powder. Line a baking sheet with parchment paper.

2. Bring almond milk to a boil in a small saucepan and reduce, uncovered, stirring constantly, until only 2 tablespoons remain. This will take about 5 minutes.

3. Reduce heat to medium, add maple crystals and salt and cook for 2 minutes. Add the almond-maca mixture and coconut oil. Stir vigorously for a few minutes.

4. Pour the fudge onto the center of the parchment, flatten, and spread it to an 8-inch square. Let the fudge rest for a few minutes. Cut into squares or diamond-shaped pieces.

Brown Rice Crispy Squares

MAKES APPROXIMATELY 12 SQUARES

Think Rice Krispy Treats, healthfully upgraded. They're ooey, gooey, crispy, a little crunchy, and perfect with a cold glass of almond milk.

GATHER

1   cup brown rice syrup

1/3 cup almond butter

1/2 teaspoon cinnamon

1/2 teaspoon vanilla extract

     Pinch of salt

3   cups brown rice cereal

8   ounces semisweet chocolate

1   teaspoon coconut oil

MAKE IT

1. In small saucepan, melt brown rice syrup over low heat until it is liquid. Stir in the almond butter until well combined. Add cinnamon, vanilla extract, and salt before removing off the heat.

2. In a medium bowl, add the brown rice cereal and slowly stream in the syrup mixture. Use a wooden spatula to gently incorporate the ingredients.

3. Transfer mixture to cutting board and use hands to form a rectangle that is approximately 2 inches thick. Cut into 12 squares.

4. In a microwave-safe bowl, melt the chocolate for 20–30 seconds, and fold in the coconut oil. Drizzle over squares, allow to set for a few minutes, and serve.

Summer Fruit Jerky

Yes, watermelon, or other fruit, can be dehydrated and made into a "meaty" jerky that has to be tasted to be believed. The key is to cut the fruit into thick strips, because it'll shrink down considerably, and to go big and bold with the flavor. It's sweet, it's savory, it's chewy, and it's amazing.

Watermelon Maple Balsamic Jerky

MAKES 12 PIECES

GATHER

1   seedless baby watermelon
    (approximately 3 pounds)

2   tablespoons maple syrup

3   tablespoons white balsamic
    vinegar

1   teaspoon olive oil

    Pinch of sea salt

MAKE IT

1. Remove rind and cut watermelon into ¹/₂-inch-thick strips.

2. Mix maple syrup, white balsamic vinegar, olive oil, and salt in a bowl.

3. Coat watermelon in marinade and arrange in a single layer on a teflex or silicone-lined dehydrator tray.

4. Dehydrate at 135°F for 16 hours, or until moisture has dissipated.

Pineapple Chipotle Barbecue Jerky

MAKES 12 PIECES

GATHER

1	large pineapple
1	teaspoon smoked paprika
1	teaspoon chili powder
1	teaspoon ground cumin
½	teaspoon garlic powder
1	tablespoon tamari (or soy sauce)
½	teaspoon maple syrup
1	teaspoon olive oil
	Pinch of sea salt

MAKE IT

1. Peel pineapple, and cut flesh into ½-inch-thick strips.

2. Mix smoked paprika, chili powder, ground cumin, garlic powder, tamari, maple syrup olive oil, and salt in bowl.

3. Coat pineapple in marinade and arrange in a single layer on a teflex or silicone-lined dehydrator tray.

4. Dehydrate at 135°F for 16 hours, or until moisture has dissipated.

Mango Sriracha Honey Jerky

MAKES 12 PIECES

GATHER

2	large mangos
1	teaspoon sriracha sauce
2	teaspoons honey
1	teaspoon maple syrup
1	teaspoon olive oil
	Pinch of sea salt

MAKE IT

1. Peel mangos and cut flesh into ½-inch-thick strips.

2. Mix sriracha, honey, maple syrup, olive oil, and salt in bowl.

3. Coat mangos in marinade and arrange in a single layer on a teflex or silicone-lined dehydrator tray.

4. Dehydrate at 135°F for 16 hours, or until moisture has dissipated.

Toasted Black Sesame Brittle

MAKES 4 SERVINGS

This brittle is gorgeous from the contrasting and striking black and white color palette.
But it's also tasty, whether on its own or crumbled on top of just about anything.
Not only are black sesame seeds delicious, they are also nutritious,
with healthy fats, fiber, iron, calcium, magnesium, and phosphorous.

GATHER

1   cup black sesame seeds

2   vanilla beans

Pinch of sea salt

1   cup unbleached cane sugar

MAKE IT

1. Line a baking sheet with a heatproof silicone mat, and set aside.

2. Add the sesame seeds to a medium pan and toast over medium heat for 2 minutes, stirring frequently. Remove from pan and allow to cool slightly.

3. Split the vanilla beans in half lengthwise and scrape out the seeds using a table knife.

4. Add vanilla seeds and salt to toasted sesame seeds, stirring to evenly distribute the vanilla and salt.

5. Place the sugar into a small saucepan, along with a candy thermometer. Heat the sugar, stirring constantly over medium heat, until the sugar becomes liquid in consistency and reaches a temperature of 295–300°F.

6. Swiftly add in sesame mixture, stirring vigorously to distribute. Quickly pour sugar mixture onto silicone mat using a spatula to spread the forming brittle to a $1/8$-inch thickness.

7. Carefully score brittle into desired shapes, taking care not to cut through the silicone mat, and refrigerate for 15–20 minutes. When firm, crack the brittle along scored lines.

Viola Blossom Honey Lollipops

MAKES 15 LOLLIPOPS

This is a magical recipe that's incredibly easy to make. We love violas and violets because they have a sweet, perfumed flavor that permeates the honey and sugar mixture. Adding the flower to the center also makes them the star and preserves them as if each pop was a prehistoric piece of petrified amber.

GATHER

15   (4-inch) lollipop sticks

15   viola blossoms

¾   cup organic cane sugar

½   cup honey

2   tablespoons water

1   teaspoon lemon extract

MAKE IT

1. Place a 2-foot wide sheet of parchment paper onto a flat surface. Line up lollipop sticks on parchment, leaving approximately 2 inches of space between sticks.

Note: if using lollipop molds, decrease proportion of honey, raising the proportion of organic cane sugar for easy removal.

2. Arrange the blossoms atop each lollipop stick. If an embedded flower is desired place the blossoms face up; if the preference is to have the flower exposed, place blossom upside down.

3. Add sugar, honey, and water to a medium pot. Mixture will foam when heated, so make sure pot has plenty of room.

4. Over medium heat, cook mixture, stirring frequently for 4–6 minutes, or until a candy thermometer reads 300–310°F.

5. Working quickly, carefully take mixture off heat and stir in lemon extract.

6. Allow mixture to stop foaming and cool for 1 minute before pouring 1-inch circles atop the arranged blossoms and sticks.

7. Allow 15–20 minutes for lollipops to set at room temperature before removing from parchment paper. Wrap in cellophane or plastic wrap for indefinite storage.

Herb Blossom Speckled Matcha and White Chocolate Bark

MAKES 10 MEDIUM-SIZE PIECES

Basil blossoms are a slightly milder version of the plant's leaves. Sprinkle them over salad, pastas, and desserts for a concentrated flavor hit. Just three ingredients make this beautiful candied bark.

GATHER

12 ounces white chocolate chips (approximately 2 cups), divided

1½ teaspoons matcha powder

1 bunch basil with blossoms (approximately 2 tablespoons), or blossoms of choice

MAKE IT

1. Set up a double boiler by bringing a small pot with 3 inches of water to a boil over a medium heat and placing a heatproof bowl on top of the pot. Line a baking sheet with parchment paper and set aside.

2. Add 1½ cups white chocolate chips in the bowl over the heat, stirring constantly with a rubber spatula, until all chocolate chips have melted.

3. Carefully remove hot bowl with melted chocolate from heat, and quickly stir in the remaining white chocolate chips, continuing to stir until all the chocolate is completely melted.

4. Pour ½ of melted chocolate onto parchment paper, using a spatula to spread into approximately ⅛-inch thickness.

5. Gradually sift in the matcha powder into the remaining chocolate, whisking vigorously to incorporate. If mixture becomes too cool to maneuver, place briefly back onto the pot with the steaming water.

6. Place dollops of the matcha chocolate onto the white chocolate layer, and use a skewer or spoon to gently drag the mixture and form swirls.

7. Sprinkle chocolate with herb blossoms and place in refrigerator for 20 minutes. Crack into pieces before serving.

Aquafaba Marshmallow Fluff

MAKES 4 CUPS

I'm not gonna lie: this is not a dessert. It's a sugary, whispery fluff
that's made from four simple ingredients. But it's pretty fantastic on top of
ice cream, a light sponge cake, or even some fresh fruit when you just want
to elevate something a little mundane into something extra special.

GATHER

1 (15-ounce) can unsalted chickpeas

½ cup maple sugar

4 teaspoons tapioca starch

Pinch of sea salt

MAKE IT

1. Strain out canned chickpea liquid or aquafaba (approximately $^3/_4$ cup). Reserve the chickpeas for future use.

2. Place aquafaba in freezer for 10–15 minutes, or until chilled.

3. In a small bowl, sift together maple sugar, tapioca starch, and salt.

4. Using stand or electric hand mixer beat aquafaba at high speed for 2–3 minutes, or until fluffy.

5. As mixer is running, add sugar mixture, tablespoon by tablespoon, until incorporated.

6. Beat for additional 3–5 minutes on high until stiff white peaks and ribbons form.

Avocado Matcha Crème Brûlée

MAKES 6 SERVINGS

This is a winner for everyone at the dinner table. It's totally vegan.
It's also gluten-free. And it has that crispy, crunchy shell that everyone loves to crack
with their spoon. We use agar flakes—a seaweed gelatin substitute—to give the brûlée
its creamy, custardy body. You can find these flakes in any health food store.

GATHER

3   tablespoons agar flakes

2   (14-ounce) cans coconut milk
    (3 ⅓ cups total)

½   cup agave syrup

1   ripe avocado, peeled

2   teaspoons matcha powder

    Pinch of sea salt

FOR THE CRACKED SHELL

⅓   cup organic cane sugar

MAKE IT

1. Add agar flakes and coconut milk to a saucepan over medium heat. Bring to a simmer, stirring occasionally, for 8–10 minutes or until the agar flakes dissolve. Cool for 5–10 minutes.

2. Add agave syrup, avocado, matcha powder, and salt to a blender, processing until smooth. Transfer to large bowl.

3. Ladle the warm coconut milk mixture into the avocado mixture and stir to incorporate.

4. Strain the avocado matcha crème to remove lumps and divide among 6 small heatproof ramekins. Refrigerate for about 60 minutes.

5. Sprinkle organic cane sugar on top of each avocado matcha crème. Use a kitchen-friendly blow torch to scorch the sugar into a cracked shell.

6. Serve immediately.

Sweet Matcha Mango Sticky Rice Rolls

MAKES 10 SPRING ROLLS

Jasmine rice adds floral notes and has a shorter cooking time than white rice, which is great if you are in a pinch. You can swap out the mango with different fruit that is in season such as fresh figs, poached pears, or other exotic varieties such as purple dragon fruit.

GATHER

1   cup jasmine rice

1¾ cups water

1   ripe mango

1   package rice paper

FOR THE SAUCE

1   (5-ounce) can coconut cream (approximately ½ cup)

2   tablespoons agave nectar

½   teaspoon matcha powder

FOR THE GARNISH

1   small bunch mint

2   tablespoons black and white sesame seeds

MAKE IT

1. Place rice and water into a pot. Bring to a simmer, cover, and cook on low heat for 15 minutes. Remove from heat and steam, covered, for 5 minutes.

2. Peel mango and cut into 10 thick, long strips. Set aside.

3. In a blender, blend together coconut cream, agave nectar, and matcha powder. Mix ½ cup of mixture with the cooked rice.

4. Rehydrate rice paper by running under water for 10 seconds. Place on cutting board and fill center with ¼ cup sticky rice, mango, mint, and sesame seeds.

5. Fold over rice paper, tucking in the sides, and roll filling tightly into a roll.

6. Repeat with remainder of ingredients. Serve with remaining sauce.

Homemade Matcha Collagen Bars

MAKES 12 BARS

Your gut will thank you for these collagen-rich dessert bars.
Be sure to use an unflavored collagen so you don't accidentally infuse it with
"lemon-lime" or "strawberry-blueberry" flavors found in collagen supplements these days.
And try substituting different nuts, such as pecans or cashews, for the crust.

GATHER

FOR THE CRUST

1 cup macadamia nuts

1 cup pitted dates

FOR THE FILLING

2 cups cashews

2 tablespoons unflavored collagen powder

1/2 cup coconut nectar

1 cup refined coconut oil

1/2 teaspoon matcha powder

1/2 cup blackberries, more for garnish

FOR THE GARNISH

1 bunch mint

MAKE IT

1. Pulse macadamia nuts and dates in a food processor until macadamia pieces are very small and mixture is sticky to the touch.

2. Transfer into an 8 x 8-inch silicone mold, or a small springform pan.

3. Soak cashews in hot water for 10 minutes.

4. Drain cashews and place in blender along with collagen powder, coconut nectar, and coconut oil.

5. Blend until smooth then remove 1 cup batter.

6. Blend remaining batter in blender with matcha powder and pour on top of crust.

7. Return reserved batter into blender, along with blackberries, and blend until smooth.

8. Pour blackberry mixture on top of matcha mixture.

9. Freeze for 1–2 hours, or until firm.

10. Cut into bars and garnish with blackberries and mint.

11. Keep extra bars frozen until ready to serve.

No-Bake Coconut-Lime Bars

MAKES 12 BARS

Five ingredients. No baking. One dish. And they have the most bright, happy
sunshine-y look to them. For people who say they don't bake,
may I present to you a blue-ribbon recipe that will become part of your repertoire.

GATHER

4   cups unsweetened large-shred
     coconut flakes, more for garnish

½   cup agave syrup

¼   cup virgin coconut oil

3   limes

     Pinch of salt

MAKE IT

1. Add coconut, agave syrup, coconut oil, and juice and zest of
   2 limes into food processor and process for 60 seconds or
   until mixture comes together.

2. Press into an 8 x 8-inch dish and top with additional coconut.

3. Cool in freezer for 15 minutes or until slightly firm and cut
   into bars.

4. Slice remaining lime into 12 thin slices and top bars.

5. Store refrigerated for up to 1 week. Bars can be frozen.

Miso-Caramel Popcorn

MAKES 8 CUPS

This recipe is our nod to when we visited Japan and shot a feature story about all the native ingredients grown and made there. We wanted to think of a recipe that elevated miso from just a hot soup, and this is what we came up with. Salty. Sweet. So satisfying. If you can't find furikake, some sesame seeds and crumbled toasted nori will work.

GATHER

½ cup organic popcorn kernels

2 tablespoons refined coconut oil

½ cup maple syrup

1 (5-ounce) can coconut cream (approximately ½ cup)

1 tablespoon miso paste

1 cup roasted salted peanuts

2 tablespoons furikake

MAKE IT

1. Add popcorn kernels and oil to a medium pot and stir to coat each kernel with oil.

2. Cover tightly with aluminum foil and cook over medium heat for 3–5 minutes, or until kernel popping slows down, carefully shaking every 30 seconds.

3. Spread popcorn into a single layer onto a large parchment-lined baking sheet and preheat oven to 325°F.

4. Add maple syrup and coconut cream to a small pan and simmer for 10 minutes. Turn off heat and stir in miso.

5. Drizzle caramel evenly over popped corn.

6. Bake mixture for 10–15 minutes, stirring once.

7. Sprinkle popcorn with peanuts and furikake and cool completely.

8. Store in airtight container for up to 1 week.

Purple Sweet Potato Pie Bars

MAKES 12 BARS

Would you believe this outrageous color comes just from the sweet potatoes?
If you have trouble finding purple taters, you can use regular orange-hued sweet potatoes.
It'll taste just as good and take on that bright, orange color instead.

GATHER

FOR THE CRUST

2   cups almond flour

⅓   cup almond butter

3   tablespoons ground flax meal

¼   cup coconut sugar

       Pinch of sea salt

¼   cup filtered water

FOR THE FILLING

4   purple sweet potatoes
       (approximately 2 pounds)

1   (14-ounce) can coconut milk
       (approximately 2 cups)

6   tablespoons agar flakes

½   cup agave nectar

2   teaspoons vanilla extract

       Pinch of sea salt

MAKE IT

1. Preheat oven to 350°F. Line bottom of an 8 x 8-inch dish with parchment paper and grease sides of dish with oil of choice.

2. In a medium bowl, mix together almond flour, almond butter, ground flax meal, coconut sugar, salt, and water until dough forms.

3. Press firmly into an even layer in greased baking dish and bake for 15 minutes.

4. Peel and chop the sweet potatoes into small pieces. Add to a pan, cover with water, bring to a boil, and cook for 10–15 minutes, or until tender. Drain well and add to blender.

5. Add agar flakes, agave nectar, vanilla extract, and salt to another pan and simmer for 10–15 minutes or until agar flakes dissolve.

6. Add agar mixture to blender and process with cooked sweet potatoes until completely smooth.

7. Pour puréed mixture on top of crust and refrigerate for a few hours to set.

8. Slice into 12 bars.

Oversized Blue Spirulina Marshmallows

MAKES 12 PIECES

Blue spirulina is a blue-green algae which grows in ponds and lakes. It's a high source of protein and has energy-boosting vitamin B. It also gives these giant, fluffy marshmallows their beautiful soft blue color. For vegans who thought they'd given up on marshmallows (traditionally, they use animal-based gelatin), this plant-based version will make them say they want s'more!

GATHER

- 2 tablespoons organic confectioners' sugar
- 1 cup aquafaba, from a (15-ounce) can of chickpeas
- 1/2 teaspoon cream of tartar
- 1 tablespoon vanilla extract
- 6 tablespoons agar flakes
- 1 1/3 cups filtered water
- 2 1/2 cups organic sugar
- 2 teaspoons blue spirulina powder

MAKE IT

1. Sprinkle bottom of a 12 x 12-inch baking dish with a thin layer of confectioners' sugar.

2. Add aquafaba and cream of tartar to a stand mixer (or alternatively, use an electric hand mixer) and beat on high for 5 minutes or until fluffy and firm peaks form.

3. Add vanilla extract, agar flakes, and water to a small pan. Bring to a simmer and cook for 10–15 minutes, or until agar flakes have dissolved. Add in organic sugar and continue to cook for 2 minutes or until dissolved.

4. Stir blue spirulina powder into a few teaspoons of water and fold into sugar mixture.

5. Take off heat, turn mixer on high, and beat hot sugar mixture slowly into whipped aquafaba.

6. Transfer mixture into sugar-coated dish.

7. Allow to set in refrigerator for 1–2 hours, or until completely chilled.

8. Loosen edges of marshmallows with a knife, place cutting board on top of dish, and gently invert. Cut into 1-inch cubes.

Sticky Toffee Baked Oatmeal

MAKES 12 BARS

A magical thing happens when you use coconut sugar and coconut milk together and let them simmer in a pan: it turns into the most wonderful toffee with a caramel-like consistency. Who thought oatmeal could be transformed into an ooey, gooey dessert?

GATHER

4   cups filtered water

4   cups rolled oats

½   cup ground flax seeds

1   cup coconut sugar

2   (14-ounce) cans coconut milk

2   tablespoons vanilla extract

1   cup pecans, extra for garnish

1   teaspoon flaky sea salt

MAKE IT

1. Preheat oven to 350°F, line inside of an 8 x 8-inch baking dish, or equivalent, with parchment paper, and grease sides lightly with oil of choice.

2. Bring water to a boil. Add oats, reduce to a simmer, and cook for 5 minutes, stirring occasionally, until oats are cooked through and have absorbed the water. Remove from heat and stir in ground flax seeds.

3. In a separate pan, add coconut sugar and coconut milk. Bring mixture to a boil and cook over medium heat for 15 minutes or mixture thickens to a caramel consistency. Remove from heat and add vanilla extract. This should yield 2 cups.

4. Chop pecans slightly and add to oats. Fold in half of the toffee mixture (approximately 1 cup) to oats and stir to combine.

5. Press oat mixture firmly into lined baking dish and bake for 20 minutes, or until firm to the touch.

6. Cool before cutting into bars and drizzle with remaining toffee mixture. Top with pecans and salt.

INDEX

METRIC CONVERSION CHART

VOLUME MEASUREMENTS		WEIGHT MEASUREMENTS		TEMPERATURE CONVERSION	
U.S.	METRIC	U.S.	METRIC	FAHRENHEIT	CELSIUS
1 teaspoon	5 ml	$\frac{1}{2}$ ounce	15 g	250	120
1 tablespoon	15 ml	1 ounce	30 g	300	150
$\frac{1}{4}$ cup	60 ml	3 ounces	90 g	325	160
$\frac{1}{3}$ cup	75 ml	4 ounces	115 g	350	180
$\frac{1}{2}$ cup	125 ml	8 ounces	225 g	375	190
$\frac{2}{3}$ cup	150 ml	12 ounces	350 g	400	200
$\frac{3}{4}$ cup	175 ml	1 pound	450 g	425	220
1 cup	250 ml	$2\frac{1}{4}$ pounds	1 kg	450	230